AND THEN
GOD GAVE
US KIDS

AND THEN GOD GAVE US KIDS

How God Uses Our Kids to Help Us Grow

TAMARA BOGGS

Kregel
Publications

And Then God Gave Us Kids: How God Uses Our Kids to Help Us Grow

© 2003 by Tamara Boggs

Published by Kregel Publications, a division of Kregel, Inc., P.O. Box 2607, Grand Rapids, MI 49501.

Cover design: John M. Lucas

Library of Congress Cataloging-in-Publication Data
Boggs, Tamara.
And then God gave us kids: how God uses our kids to help us grow / by Tamara Boggs.
      p. cm.
   1. Parenting—Religious aspects—Christianity. 2. Parents—Religious life. I. Title.
BV4529.B63   2003
242'.645—dc21   2002154869

ISBN 0-8254-2093-8

Printed in the United States of America
03 04 05 06 07 / 5 4 3 2 1

CONTENTS

CONTENTS

ℐNTRODUCTION

MY SISTER TONYA IS a remarkable woman. She's an organized home manager, a loving wife and mother, and she homeschools her six children. Is she living in God's will for her life? She believes so, and so do I.

Yet parents sometimes find it difficult to experience spiritual connection to, and confirmation of, God while dealing with the demands and distractions of parenting. A recent phone conversation between Tonya and me illustrates this.

"Tamara," said Tonya, "all of my life I've heard about Jesus loving me, but it's not the same as knowing it. Excuse me. . . .

"*Daniel, I don't know. . . . I'll try to get to it before I go to bed tonight. . . .* Sorry about that."

"No problem."

"Anyway . . . I think I'm having a kind of midlife crisis. I'm just not satisfied to live on this level of relationship with God. Just a minute.

"*Get up. . . . I don't think lying on your brother's book is the best way to do that. . . .* OK, I'm back."

"Sure," I said. "Have you ever read Brother Lawrence's *The Practice of the Presence of God?* He was a monk in a monastery, of course, and didn't have six children, but—"

"Excuse me again. *Ruth, stop! Don't destroy that book!* Sorry."

"That's all right. Anyway, Brother Lawrence didn't have

children but he had long days of routine grunge work to do, and he learned how to experience God in the midst of—

"Boys, stop wrestling! Get up off the floor, so you won't even be tempted. If you do it again, I'm going to send you out to move the woodpile. . . . Yes, in the rain. Sigh. Sounds like a good book. I need something . . . *No, take your book and sit in your father's chair. . . . Yes, until I get off the phone.* I'm sorry."

"That's all right—been there. Well, if you get a chance, it's worth a read. It's short, and it's very encouraging that you can experience God's love and real presence if—"

"Oh dear . . . are you going to need an ice pack for that? I'm sorry, sis, I need to go."

And so goes the life of a parent. We long for relationship with God, yet time to focus on a spiritual life is a rare commodity. So how does God's will for our spiritual well-being play out during our parenting years? Surely God didn't intend for our souls to wither away amidst a desert of dirty diapers and carpool exhaust.

Underneath all of the important roles and relationships of parenting—beyond all we *do*—each of us is a unique person treasured by God as his child. Just as we invest our energy, time, and love in our children, God as a perfect parent invests his unending love and inexhaustible energy in each of our lives, our growth, and our spiritual well-being.

While telling stories about God's kingdom life, Jesus quoted the prophet Isaiah in regard to his listeners: "Though seeing, they do not see; though hearing, they do not hear or understand" (Matt. 13:13). Jesus said, "He who has ears to hear, let him hear" (Mark 4:9). Was Jesus implying that we humans often miss the kingdom of God when it's right in front of us? Do we fail to notice the truths, the lessons, the blessings in plain view all around us? Are the kingdom stories that Jesus wants us as parents to hear and see, about our children? When

God gives us kids, God offers to write on our hearts the countless truths contained in the parables of parenthood.

Jesus said, "If you, then, though you are evil, know how to give good gifts to your children, how much more will your Father in heaven give good gifts to those who ask him!" (Matt. 7:11). Could it be that, during the parenting years, the special gifts God wants us to see and receive are our children?

Through our experience as parents who love our children, we can begin to understand in the deepest level of our hearts how much God must love and treasure *us* as *his* children. Simply recognizing and absorbing this underlying love and delight that God has for us can release a stream of refreshing spiritual life into the wilderness of parenting demands. This depth of understanding comes *because* we are parents not *in spite of* being parents.

During the parenting years, the demands of those who depend upon us take much of our time. But it requires only a moment to take notice of your children, yourself, and your relationship to them. The trick is perspective, that is, taking the moment to notice—having "ears to hear and eyes to see" God's living model—Jesus' daily spiritual story lessons for us as we live in our families!

Living with these ears and eyes open sometimes means receiving the gift of our children as an example of how to be *childlike* as Jesus invited us to do, in order to enter the kingdom of heaven (Luke 18:16–17; Matt. 18:2–4). Having ears and eyes open also means recognizing, through our children, the childish ways we need to put away, those areas in which we need maturing (1 Cor. 13:11). At other times this eyes-open perspective will give deeper insight into the nature of God's relationship to us as our heavenly parent. At still other times it means insight into living in relationship to our brothers and sisters as children in God's family.

The following stories and reflections trace my journey, following this path with eyes and ears open. As in my previous book, *Children*

Are a Blessing from the Lord: Learning God's Wisdom Through Our Children, I suggest that God gives us kids not as a detriment but as an enrichment to our relationship with him.

My prayer is that through God's gift of children, your relationship with your heavenly Father will become as real as your child's breathless grin, the musty aroma of sweaty child hair, melted M&Ms deposited in your palms, and bear hugs at bedtime.

$\mathcal{M}$EET MY FAMILY

As I complete the writing of *And Then God Gave Us Kids,* I realize that my children have grown considerably since the first stories in this book about Nathaniel's infancy. So, it may be helpful to introduce our family in order to give you a context for these narratives.

Nathaniel and Christiana are now teenagers and Hannah is eleven. Don and I celebrated our nineteenth wedding anniversary this past summer. Don is a university professor and also runs an Internet bookstore, selling books on the history of spaceflight. At the end of a workday, however, Don has always laid aside his stack of to-do papers in order to join our family at the dinner table. His dry wit keeps me laughing and the children at least smiling politely.

Nathaniel is our quiet analyst and passionate game player. Before the age of four he had worn out two decks of Sesame Street Uno cards, and so at age five moved on to checkers, Yahtzee, Rook, and (to our surprise) chess. He continues to amaze us with his insight not only into the complexities of chess, but also into the game of life and faith.

Christiana is the colorful flower of tangible love in our family garden of abundant intellectual foliage. She was a high-need baby and toddler. Trying to understand and deal with her intense needs often brought us to the ends of our intellectual and emotional resources—and running to the feet of our heavenly Father. Since entering the public school system in second grade (we homeschooled our children until then), she has been in special education classes for the mildly mentally handicapped.

Christiana has been in a variety of physical and speech therapies since she was eighteen months old, but was not identified as mildly autistic until she was nine. This diagnosis explained many of her peculiar behaviors, such as her daily routines of lengthy sessions on the backyard swing, and her role-playing to process her day, using school papers and clothing items to represent her classroom of students. Understanding her autism has also helped us to build a bridge to her world of concrete literalism, limited interests, and social challenges. Her unique perspective has taught us much about making our Christian walk real.

Hannah is our artist, with an inquisitive intellect and a passion for piano and singing. She can't walk by our piano at home without dropping whatever she is doing and stopping to play. This is wonderful, except for the collection of school papers, jackets, and sundry items that accumulate next to the piano. I don't have to ask her to practice, but I often ask her to pick up. The combination of Hannah's challenging questions and her gift in music have helped us not to take anything for granted—especially our faith—and to enjoy all the beauty and blessings in our lives.

These three children of God have been our teachers, motivators, and inspirers. Don and I thank our heavenly Father for the insights we have gained over these past sixteen years through his gift of our beloved family.

AND THEN
GOD GAVE
US KIDS

ᏩIVING BIRTH

Jesus answered, "I tell you the truth, no one can enter the kingdom of God unless he is born of water and the Spirit. Flesh gives birth to flesh, but the Spirit gives birth to spirit. . . . For God so loved the world that he gave his one and only Son, that whoever believes in him shall not perish but have eternal life."

—John 3:5–6, 16

Let us fix our eyes on Jesus, the author and perfecter of our faith, who for the joy set before him endured the cross.

—Hebrews 12:2

I SAT ON THE BED in the dim light listening to the silence, staring at the waiting crib. A movement within my womb, but not of my will, drew my attention to the growing life within. I stretched my back muscles and repositioned myself on the bed to give my compressed diaphragm more room to draw breath.

Two weeks until the due date of my first born; I felt excited and apprehensive. I had studied my baby's day-by-day growth chart. Psalm 139:13 came to mind—"You knit me together in my mother's womb." The little one moved again as if to affirm my thoughts. I rubbed the distended skin of a new bump on my tummy. Was it an elbow or a foot? It would be a foot if baby was turned head down—hopefully a foot.

My abdomen hardened. A Braxton-Hicks contraction, but this one lasted. "Ouch."

I lumbered out to the dining room where Don was working on the computer. I laid down on the couch. After a few minutes my abdomen hardened again. A few minutes later, again.

"Are you all right, honey?" Don asked.

I didn't answer right away.

Don examined me from across the room.

"I think I'll go fix myself some hot dogs."

It was only five o'clock, early for supper. "Why?"

"I don't think I'll have time to eat later."

Two hours later, I lay on my side in birthing-room two, trying to relax and breathe deeply and slowly while my uterus worked to open the birth canal. I gazed at the peaceful ocean scene—I'd brought it with me as a focus object to help me control my breathing and relaxation. I couldn't believe this was labor. Everyone said it would be so painful.

Don stood next to me, holding a clipboard and etching our life history onto the hospital paperwork. Breathe. Relax. Focus. Breathe. Relax. . . . Gasp! My uterus clenched into a knot, and a tremor of agony radiated through my body, taking my breath away. I tried to stay calm. I tried to breathe. I wanted to scream, to stand up and run away from the excruciating pain. But I couldn't say a word. I squeezed my eyes shut. Moaning and panting I grabbed Don's belt.

"What's wrong, honey?" He put the clipboard on the table next to the bed and picked up my ocean picture.

"Ohhh," I wailed. The contraction abated, and I took deep breaths of relief. "I think . . . I'm in . . . tran . . . sition."

Another wave of pain, sharper than the last, gripped me. I tensed against the onslaught and instantly realized my mistake as the agony doubled. I tried to relax. I stared at Don and groaned. In response, he held my focus picture in front of my face. My grip on his belt tightened. Don jumped back, grabbing my wrist as I caught some of his flesh with my fingernails.

The contraction eased and I shoved the picture away from my face, sending it skittering across the floor. Don's brow creased with helpless inadequacy and rejected affection. That expression would have brought compassion and repentance from me in any other situation.

"Sorry . . . not now," I panted. I released his stomach and closed my eyes, bracing for the next onslaught.

So *this* is labor. Another contraction threatened. Feelings of self-preservation surfaced. *I don't want to have a baby! I quit! If I had only known!* The consuming pain erased all further extraneous thoughts.

Several hours later, I held my first born, Nathaniel, in my arms. His wrinkled little-old-man face and his bright, searching eyes made him look wise, as if he knew the answers to all of life's questions. He was indeed wondrously made, a messenger delivered from the presence of God to bless us with tidings of great joy.

The pain? I was relieved that no one had given me a choice to back out of the birthing process at the time of greatest suffering. In the midst of the agony, I had not understood as I did now—Nathaniel was worth it!

Reflections

Birthing is such a painful process! Yet God, our heavenly parent, loved us so much that he sent his son, Jesus Christ, who chose to bear the agonizing pain of labor on the cross so that our souls might be born into new life. May this reality sink deeply into our hearts, so that we might love God all the more and praise him and serve him with great joy.

Prayer

Dear God, remembering the elation of love I felt after my babies were born, I can barely imagine the delight that overflows from your heart, your endless and perfect love for me as your child. May I rest as an infant in your arms, staring with adoration into your eyes, knowing I am loved like an infant for simply being who I am. I am utterly dependent upon you. Thank you, Jesus, for going through your labor of love so that I could be born again of the Spirit as your child. Amen.

A BOUNTIFUL SUFFICIENCY

Like newborn babies, crave pure spiritual milk, so that by it you may grow up in your salvation, now that you have tasted that the Lord is good.

—1 Peter 2:2–3

Pray continually.

—1 Thessalonians 5:17

I LOOPED ON MY favorite earrings and glanced at my watch. Twenty 'til ten. Good. My first meeting with the mom's breast-feeding support group was at ten. I might be on time for a change. I stood for a moment in front of the mirror and frowned at my chubby middle. I guess I shouldn't expect to have my extra weight off only four weeks after delivery. At least I was out of my robe and I had makeup on. I felt like I'd spent most of the last month in the rocking chair, nursing Nathaniel. Maybe today I'd find out why he nursed so much.

Nathaniel fussed in the next room. I'd hoped to sneak him into the car seat while he was napping. I lifted him out of his crib.

"Hello, sweetie. Did you have a good nap?"

His cry stopped, and he turned his head toward my chest, mouthing my blouse. I repositioned him on my shoulder, but he whimpered and tossed his head back and forth.

"You can't be hungry. You ate just two hours ago."

I draped him face forward over my arm and checked his diaper. "Let's change you."

Nathaniel wiggled and arched his back on the bathroom counter. He turned his head from side to side, mouth and eyes wide open.

"You *do* want to nurse. Well, you're just going to have to wait."

We headed out the door with ten minutes to get across town. My cooing and singing did little to quiet Nathaniel's oratorio of hunger from the backseat. By the time I pulled into the community center my nerves were wearing thin. I unfastened the buckles on the car seat and lifted my screaming infant into my arms. His volume dropped to the pained whimper of a trust betrayed, a hope renewed. He brushed his mouth back and forth across my shoulder in an emphatic plea for mother's milk. I glanced at my watch, debating whether to nurse him in the car or go into the meeting. The notice had said babies were welcome.

When I walked into the meeting room, the first thing I noticed was a mother who sat in the circle of chairs and nursed her baby. She was chatting with a friend as if she didn't notice the baby in her lap attached and guzzling. Nathaniel whined and wiggled in my arms. One of the mothers walked over.

"Sounds like you have a hungry one there. Feel free to nurse him. None of us mind. I'm Alison, one of the leaders."

"Thank you. I'm Tamara Boggs. I can't believe he's really hungry. I fed him just a couple of hours ago."

"He's still a little one. It's normal for some babies to nurse every couple of hours for the first months. You know, he benefits from your immunities, and he needs to be close for emotional growth, too. He's not a cow." She laughed.

I nodded, not sure what to say.

She put her hand on my shoulder. "I mean, he's a human baby with emotional as well as physical needs. He'll slow down when he's ready."

I found a seat and cradled Nathaniel in my arms. Soon he was gulping milk, his eyes closed. His tiny fingers gripped and released the edge of my blouse and then relaxed. I made a tent over Nathaniel, pulling a soft yellow blanket over my shoulder. In a moment the flow of milk slowed, and he heaved a deep sigh between swallows. The women around me settled into the circle.

I peeked under the blanket. Nathaniel's blue eyes gazed at me with intense interest. His forehead wrinkled and his eyes widened as if he were trying to better focus on me—his source of all goodness, the center of his universe, this extension of himself. I smiled, not wanting to look away. No, he wasn't a cow. If he needed me to be close and nurse often for another month, I didn't mind. There was nothing more important than helping this little one grow strong and healthy. In just a few months he wouldn't need me to nurse him at all.

"Today we'll be talking about the benefits of breast-feeding," Alison said.

I relaxed into my seat, contented.

Reflections

Newborns need to nurse long and often. And when we are newborn in Christ, we need frequent, lengthy feedings from Jesus for spiritual growth, emotional attachment, and immunity from spiritual disease. Sometimes we let less important activities—especially those that others press upon us—infringe upon our spiritual nurturing time. Recognizing that time with our heavenly parent is an eternal-life necessity, not just a selfish want, gives us permission to make our spiritual feeding times a higher priority.

You wouldn't let your children go hungry. Your heavenly parent loves you and longs for you to be spiritually fed, growing, healthy, and content!

Prayer

Dear God, I will never outgrow my need for your ever-present nourishment. When I go through growth spurts in my spiritual life, help me to allow myself to feed from your Word and spend extra time with you. Make me sensitive to the needs of newborn believers, help me to encourage them to live close to you and drink in your nourishing love and the love of your family. Amen.

$\mathcal{F}$IXING BABIES

Never will I leave you; never will I forsake you.
—Hebrews 13:5

The Lord is near. Do not be anxious about anything.
—Philippians 4:5–6

BEFORE DON ENTERED our bedroom, carrying Nathaniel, the baby's cries woke me.

"Honey," Don whispered, cradling the squirming infant above me, "maybe he needs to nurse."

I rolled over and looked at the clock—five A.M.

"I don't think so," I closed my eyes and rearranged my pillow under my head. "He nursed just over an hour ago. Is he dry?"

"Yes."

"Maybe he has gas. Try pumping his legs."

"I did."

"Try singing him a song. Babies are supposed to like soothing bass voices."

"I've gone through 'Old Man River' and 'Swing Low Sweet Chariot' a dozen times. Are you sure he isn't hungry? Maybe he's having a growth spurt."

"He's always having a growth spurt." I sighed. "All right. I'll see what I can do."

I swung my legs over the side of the bed and rubbed my face into wakefulness.

"Give him to me." I held out my arms to receive my sweet bundle of early-morning joy. Don headed to his side of the bed and flopped. The needs of our first-born son sometimes defied logic, and Don wasn't yet used to that.

"I don't get it," I said. "We learn all of these neat things to take care of our baby and half the time they don't work."

Nathaniel started rooting to nurse as soon as I held him close.

"I wonder if he really needs to nurse, or if he just thinks he does because he's uncomfortable. If he has gas, feeding will just make it worse."

I turned Nathaniel away from me and held him forward to face over my hand so that he would have pressure on his tummy. He stopped crying and relaxed into the rhythm of my bounce.

"What did you do?" said Don. "Why did he stop crying?"

"I don't know. Nothing you haven't already done. He's a baby. He doesn't always play by our rules. I think I'll go and walk him for a while." I stood up and headed toward the door.

"Good luck," said Don as I turned off the light.

"Thanks."

Reflections

When we jump in too soon to fix our children's struggles—or the problems of those whom we love—we are often simply revealing our own fears. When we're feeling helpless, we sometimes need to ask God for the faith not to act, but just *be* with our distressed loved one. When we listen to those we care about, with prayer-filled understanding and compassion, we help them learn faith during the hard times in life— faith in themselves and in their relationship to God.

Prayer

Dear God, help me to know that I don't always have to fix my children or any of my loved ones. Help me to truly see them and listen to their hearts. Help me to know that loving sometimes means just being with someone, as you promised to be with me in my struggles. As my children grow, help me to be a safe and loving person to whom they can bring their pain and fear, without their feeling that I'll be upset by their searching and struggling. Above all, help me to put my children and all those I care about into your hands. When I don't know what the solution is—you do! Thank you for the peace of your faithful presence. Amen.

$\mathcal{S}$EEING GOD'S FACE

Now we see but a poor reflection as in a mirror; then we shall see face to face. Now I know in part; then I shall know fully, even as I am fully known.
—1 Corinthians 13:12

"YOU GO ON TO BED, I'll wait up for David," my sister Tonya whispered to me. She nestled into the couch cushions with her eleven-month-old baby, Stephen.

Tonya and her five children had driven from Virginia to rendezvous with our family early in the week at a secluded mountain cabin in West Virginia. Her husband, David, planned to join us for the weekend, and we had expected him earlier in the evening. Now, it was dark. On both of our minds were the narrow dirt roads and four switchbacks that led to the top of our backwoods paradise.

I started up the stairs to my bedroom, not wanting to waken Stephen. He'd finally fallen asleep after an hour of on-and-off nursing. The cabin stairs creaked. Stephen jerked his head up and, with a grunt, struggled off Tonya's lap.

"It looks like I'm going to be up a little longer, anyhow." Tonya sat forward and handed Stephen a drink coaster to play with as he steadied himself against the coffee table.

"Sorry," I said. "I'm sure David won't be too much longer. These West Virginia roads can take a while to navigate. Since Stephen is up, I'll dress for bed and come back down."

Tonya smiled and nodded.

I brushed my teeth and walked down the hall to the window on the road side of the cabin. I squinted my eyes as if it would help me see further through the thick country darkness. A faint glow flashed, faded, and then reappeared—headlights bobbing up and down the hilly final stretch.

Thank you, Lord, I sighed in relief and headed back down the stairs. Tonya and I got to the front door at the same time.

"Do you want me to hold Stephen?" I held out my arms. Stephen leaned against Tonya's shoulder.

"That's OK, I'll take him out to see his daddy."

"You better take a flashlight. It's dark out there."

"I've got one." She held up the light and flicked on the switch.

I waited inside for them to come in, listening to the muffled words of their happy greeting. The car doors slammed and I opened the front door for the weary traveler.

"So you found us. Welcome!"

David carried a briefcase in one hand and Stephen in the other arm. "At last. I didn't think I'd ever get here." Stephen leaned on David's shoulder, his face dominated by a delighted grin.

"Are you happy to see Daddy?" I asked. He gave a slight nod and reached an arm across David's chest, attempting to wrap his father in a possessive hug.

"Time for bed, Stephen," said Tonya, coming through the door with David's bag. "David, will you take him up to bed? I'll be there in a minute."

"Certainly," said David. The father and son, happy to be reunited, headed up the stairs.

Tonya watched them until they were out of sight. "It's funny," she said. "When David first got out of the car, Stephen wouldn't go to him. Then I shined the light on David's face and Stephen reached for him. I guess he didn't recognize him in the dark. He just wasn't sure until he saw his father's face."

Reflections

We will never know God fully in this life. In the fourteenth through sixteenth chapters of the gospel of John, however, Jesus tells us that if we have seen him we have seen the Father. He tells us, too, that if we wait upon the Holy Spirit we can gain further understanding and ongoing experience of the glory and guidance of God.

We can rest in the reassurance that the difficulties of this life are only for a time. We have a promise and a hope to hold when times are hard and understanding is dim—one day we will be home, where tears and fears are no more, joy and delight are forever ours, leaning into the loving arms of our heavenly father.

Prayer

Dear God, some day I will see you face to face. Help me to learn what you look like, so that on that day I will know you even as I am now known by you. Jesus came to show us your love, so as I read about him, help me to recognize the welcome of your outstretched arms. Help me to recognize the majesty of your brow in the mountain ranges and all the mighty works of your creation. Help me to see your smile in the smiles of my brothers and sisters as we serve each other. Help me to recognize the love in your gaze as I experience the holiness of your presence in moments of revelation. I am peering through the darkness of this world, missing you and waiting for the day when the light will shine on your face, and in delight I will go to you in an eternal embrace. In Jesus' name, Amen.

$\mathcal{J}$ASTE AND SEE

Taste and see that the LORD is good;
blessed is the man who takes refuge in him.

—Psalm 34:8

MY LITTLE BOY Nathaniel—it was hard to believe that he was already a year old. He was our precious only son, cute and sensitive, with an intelligent gaze that seemed to take in every detail of his world. I had researched all the latest parenting suggestions, maximizing every developmental toy and tool we could manage. One topic harped on in the literature was the evils of refined sugar (or at least too much refined sugar). So I had faithfully nursed my infant and had blended his baby food from fresh fruits and veggies. He had eaten no cookies, no ice cream, no donuts—and no cake. But today was his first birthday.

"So, Don," I said, "what do you think? Should we have a cake or not? Nathaniel has never had refined sugar. The practical side of me says that having a banana would be just the same to him, but—"

"—but it's not quite the traditional first birthday celebration to remember," Don finished my thought. "I'm sure a little sugar isn't going to hurt. Why don't you go get a cake."

Thirty minutes later, I squeezed through the front door carrying a bag of groceries and a cake box. I busied myself putting away the groceries. "Don, would you bring Nathaniel in, please?"

"Sure." Don flew Nathaniel into the room with a cartoonlike fanfare, and the little boy grinned as his daddy landed him in his high chair.

"Here he is, ladies and gentlemen, the man of the hour! The one and only, Nathaniel Boggs!"

"Yaay!" I snapped on the tray and tied his bib around his neck.

Don glanced at the cake box on the table. "Time for cake!"

"Sort of." I opened the white box and pulled out a chocolate cake with fluffy chocolate icing—the size of an éclair. "Look what Mommy got for you. Just enough for the birthday boy."

I set the cake on the table and opened a nearby drawer to grab a birthday candle. Don picked up the camera.

Nathaniel sighted a banana sitting on the counter. He gestured toward it, babbling "b" sounds, which meant, "Not in the drawer, Mom; the banana is over there."

As I lit the candle, we sang, "Happy birthday to you, happy birthday to you, happy birthday, dear Nathaniel. Happy birthday to you!"

I eased the little cake nearer to the birthday boy but just out of reach in case he tried to touch the glowing candle. But Nathaniel didn't reach for the cake. Instead, he wrinkled his brow and pressed back in his high chair. With his wispy hair hardly covering his round head, Nathaniel looked more like a crotchety old man than an excited one-year-old.

"It's all right, sweetie."

I blew out the candle and sat the cake on Nathaniel's tray. He looked at me and then Don, but still didn't touch the cake.

Don sat down on the bench opposite Nathaniel and shot another picture.

"See, it's all right." I took off the candle and scooted the cake nearer to him, then placed his baby spoon on the tray. "Try a bite."

Nathaniel might not know the word *cake* but *bite* had been in his vocabulary for some time. He raised his eyebrows and leaned down to examine the cake.

"That's it. Take a bite."

Nathaniel pinched the edge of the cake with his right hand and then opened and closed his fingers, smashing a miniscule sample of icing and cake between his fingers as if testing the texture. Then he inserted his left index finger into the middle of the cake and took a crumb to his lips to taste it.

He grinned.

Don continued to click off pictures.

I sat down on the bench. "Enjoy."

Nathaniel picked up his spoon. Both hands and spoon pounced on the cake with enthusiasm. He was like an explorer who'd stumbled upon a remarkable discovery. During the next ten minutes Nathaniel smashed, smeared, ate—and wore—the pretty petit four, converting it into crumbs and sugar paste. He himself transformed from a cautious skeptic into a giggly, babbling, tray-pounding, happy-birthday kid with a new favorite food.

All it had taken was a taste.

Reflections

It's easier and safer to observe than to experience. When we experience, we're vulnerable to disappointment, to hurt or irritation, to liking and then losing. A relationship with God can also seem like risky business. If we're not diligent in our Christian lives, we can find ourselves settling into a safe religion, observing instead of experiencing a dynamic relationship with God. But when we taste of God, sometimes in new ways, sometimes in precious familiar ways, we find that God is good, sweet, and nurturing, a reason for enjoyment and celebration.

Prayer

Dear God, may I reach out and touch you today, and then take the risk of drawing you into myself, tasting of your goodness. When I seek for relationship with you, then I also will enjoy the sweetness of your

Spirit and your love, your joy and goodness, your patience, kindness, faithfulness, your strength and wisdom. I praise you today, Lord! May I feast upon all that you are and see that you are indeed good! Through Jesus and in his name, Amen.

PYRAMIDS AND SANDBOXES

*When I was a child, I talked like a child, I thought like
a child, I reasoned like a child. When I became a man, I
put childish ways behind me.*

—1 Corinthians 13:11

I SAT ON THE EDGE of my seat as the hired driver pressed the van in starts and stops through the heavy traffic of Cairo, Egypt. Riding on my back in a child carrier was Nathaniel, almost two years old.

High rise office buildings and modern hotels contrasted with the ragged, makeshift awnings stretched above the huddled beggars and vendors who lined the crowded streets. As we pushed our way toward the pyramids and sphinx at Giza, acrid odors of sweat and sewage mixed with the delicious aromas of baking bread and falafel frying over open cooking fires.

I was a sightseer, riding with my husband and several college students. They were producing a video promoting a mission organization's Middle Eastern work.

Nathaniel flexed and straightened his legs in a bouncing rhythm, causing my back muscles to tense and knot against the pull of his twenty-eight pounds.

"Nathaniel, please stop." I reached back and pulled his chubby legs out from under him.

A donkey, driven hard to keep up with motor traffic, pulled a cart loaded with watermelons across the road in front of us.

I pointed. "Look at the donkey."

Nathaniel leaned over to get a better view out the window, and I regretted the suggestion. I wanted him in the carrier because a boy who explored his world by putting hand to mouth would be susceptible to the myriad of intestinal diseases found in Egypt. But after our first day my back muscles were strained and sore. As we parked next to the camel herders in the visitor's lot at Giza, I tightened the waist strap to carry as much weight on my hips as possible. I bent low, exiting the van, so as to not beam Nathaniel in the head.

The crew unloaded the videotaping equipment and we hiked toward ancient wonders. As we approached the Great Pyramid, I felt smaller and smaller. No picture could have prepared me for standing next to the massive slabs that made up its foundation. Each stone was my height and then some. I tried to comprehend the building of such an amazing structure. Placing my hand on the hot, pale stone, worn rough with age, wind, and vandalism, I pondered the persons who had quarried this very stone six thousand years earlier.

Nathaniel's feet pushed into my back, and his tug at my ponytail jerked me out of contemplation. He pointed to the camels standing nearby waiting for tourists to pay for a ride. He mumbled something about the word *go*.

"We'll see the camels later with Papa."

Nathaniel rocked back and forth. "Go. Go."

I'd been standing still too long for him and he wanted a change of scenery. Wandering over to the shade of a palm tree, I unbuckled the waist strap and eased the pack off my back. After I'd pulled Nathaniel from his confinement he yanked my hand, leading me back toward the pyramid. Perhaps he *had* noticed the impressive structure after all. I followed him, but when he cleared the shade of the palm he stopped, squatted down, and grabbed two handfuls of sand. I started to intervene and then changed my mind. No disease could survive in this scorching heat. Nathaniel watched intently as the tiny grains trickled from his fists. He opened his gritty fingers and turned to show me, wearing a big grin.

"All gone," he piped, then plunged his fingers once again into the pile and repeated the game.

I placed a hand on either side of my back and stretched. The wondrous, ancient structure loomed above us, but Nathaniel was oblivious to both its ability to inspire awe and to its significance. It would be many years before he would look up and see the pyramids.

Reflections

All children, even God's children, need to have safe and happy play times to grow into healthy adults. But as Christians, we need to be aware of the difference between healthy child-likeness and immature childishness. The former encourages growth, and the latter keeps us focused on our miniscule piece of time and place where we miss God's eternal vision.

Prayer

Dear God, I am your little child. Some days I play in the sand, delighting in simplicity and joy and the comfort of repetition in my spiritual life. You watch over me there and keep me safe. Thank you.

As I grow in you, help me to look up from my simplistic ways and see what you have wrought through the ages—works born of labor and sufferings beyond my imaginings, connecting me to all who have come before me in your kingdom.

I am your child in both attitudes. Make me sensitive to your call, feeling both the joy and safety of playing in the sand, as well as the sense of connectedness that comes from pondering the pyramids. Amen.

TRUSTING PAPA

So do not fear, for I am with you;
do not be dismayed, for I am your God.
I will strengthen you and help you;
I will uphold you with my righteous right hand.

—Isaiah 41:10

My help comes from the LORD,
the Maker of heaven and earth.
He will not let your foot slip—
he who watches over you will not slumber;
indeed, he who watches over Israel
will neither slumber nor sleep.

—Psalm 121:2–4

I STRODE THROUGH the house, headed to the backyard with my blow-dryer. My father had taught me the trick of using a blow-dryer to get a charcoal fire going. It looked odd, but always got the job done in a hurry—and I was in a hurry. The guests for my niece's wedding rehearsal dinner were arriving, and I needed to get the food on the table.

Hannah, our nine-month-old, fussed as I passed by the living room. I'd left her in Aunt Susan's capable hands, but Aunt Susan lived out of state and Hannah had only been with her once before. So Hannah wasn't as sure as I about Aunt Susan's qualifications. But I had to get this fire going, even if Hannah yowled in protest. I walked on through the kitchen and out the back door.

Guests were milling about the yard, talking. I turned on the blow-dryer. A red glow and then orange flames rewarded me. Aunt Susan appeared at the back door, Hannah squirming in her arms. I shut off the wonder dryer.

Hannah put out her arms as Susan came near.

"All right. Come here." I picked up Hannah and she patted my cheek with a chubby hand as if scolding me for leaving her with a stranger.

"Sorry, Susan," I said. "I guess Hannah doesn't know you very well yet."

"That's OK," said Susan. "She'll get to know me better as she gets older."

I went back inside, balancing Hannah on my hip. "Let's see—the buns, condiments, and chips are out on the table. I almost forgot—lettuce and tomato."

Sally, the bride-to-be, walked into the kitchen. "Is there anything I can do to help?"

"I need some slicing done. But, I hate to keep you in here when your friends are outside. How about if you take Hannah out and I'll finish up."

"Sure." Sally put her arms out and smiled at Hannah. Hannah leaned into my chest.

"Come on, Hannah, you know Cousin Sally. You've played with her lots of times." I pried Hannah free and handed her over. She started to whimper, reaching back toward me. "I'm sure she'll be all right when you get her outside."

Sally took her and headed to the backyard. "We'll be fine."

I pulled the tomatoes and lettuce out of the fridge and put them on the cutting board. Then I stepped into the living room to look out the window at how Hannah was doing. Sally was offering Hannah a potato chip; Hannah turned away.

Babies are emotional barometers. They always know when I'm tense. Oh, well, she'll live through this. She's safe with Sally.

A few minutes later, I pushed through the back door with my plate of lettuce and tomatoes in hand. I glanced over at the charcoal. Good. It was ready for the hamburgers. Hannah wasn't crying. Great. I looked around to locate her.

Hannah was not safely wrapped in Cousin Sally's or Aunt Susan's arms. She was standing seven feet above the ground, perched atop Papa's big hands. His arms were fully extended, with his hands wrapped around Hannah's thighs while she balanced above his head like an acrobat. With her arms slightly raised to keep her equilibrium, Hannah teetered back and forth, a gleeful grin lighting up her rosy cheeks. I stood still, holding my breath, as if my slightest movement might upset her balance and send her tumbling to the ground.

Don had done this trick with all of our children. No one had ever fallen, but I had never gotten comfortable with his defying gravity with my babies. After what seemed hours, Don pulled Hannah down and cradled her in the crook of his arm. She laughed, enjoying the quick ride from her lookout station.

I put the tomato plate on the serving table then walked over to Don. A sudden urge to hold Hannah had come over me. "Some trick you've got there." Hannah smiled and kicked her feet, making no gesture for me to take her.

Don said, "Relax, honey. She's perfectly safe. She's with her Papa."

I couldn't figure out how Hannah could feel safe seven feet off the ground—when she didn't feel secure wrapped in a loving relative's arms. But this time I took *my* stress reading from Hannah. Her contented, shining eyes told me all I needed to know—she knew she was safe in her Papa's hands.

Reflections

God is strong and able to sustain us. It helps us to realize God's promise to be our refuge if we meditate on God going with us and holding us up throughout the day. If we envision God going ahead of us into the places we will go, providing us with the strength, love, and wisdom we'll need, it can help us to face with peace and assurance the time, the tasks, and the people in our upcoming day. God is our ever-loving place of rest and safety.

Prayer

Dear God, past experiences of falling down emotionally and morally have left me afraid of risk. I will fail sometimes as I try to do your work. My emotions, my pride, my things, even certain relationships may crash to the ground, but you will never let me fall. Help me to know that I can trust you, that you will hold me up when I feel like I'm in a precarious place. In your love, which is always attentive, I am safe. Thank you. Amen.

$\mathcal{P}$LAYING ROOK IN HEAVEN

All these people were still living by faith when they died. . . . Therefore, . . . we are surrounded by such a great cloud of witnesses.

—Hebrews 11:13; 12:1

Brothers [and sisters], we do not want you to be ignorant about those who fall asleep, or to grieve like the rest of men, who have no hope.

—1 Thessalonians 4:13

Jesus said to her, "I am the resurrection and the life. He who believes in me will live, even though he dies; and whoever lives and believes in me will never die. Do you believe this?"

—John 11:25–26

"YOU'VE GOT TWO THREES, a four, a one, and a five." Above the highway noises of whistling wind and whining tires, Nathaniel informed me of the numbers on my Yahtzee dice.

The eight-hour trip to Alabama for my Grandpa Clemens's funeral was almost all mindless, interstate driving. I kept my eyes on the road and my hands on the steering wheel, but gave the leftover portion of my attention to Nathaniel, my five-year-old game wizard.

"Let's see," I said. "Do I have my threes yet?"

"No, you still need your threes."

"How about my large straight?"

"No, you don't have that either."

"Roll one of the threes and let's see if I can get the two for a large straight."

"But, Mama, you've got to get at least four threes or you'll lose your bonus thirty-five."

"If I don't get my large straight, I'll lose forty points."

Nathaniel rubbed the travel die roller across his hand and then popped the loose die into place before turning it over. "Sorry, you got another three. You could still go for your threes, you know."

I glanced over at Nathaniel. His lips were drawn tight with concern for my well being—easy for the boy who already had his Yahtzee, his large straight, and his upper bonus scored.

"All right," I said, "Pop out everything but the threes and roll again."

The dice clacked and whirred as he tumbled the roller across his leg. "Pop, pop, pop" into place. "You got your threes! Four of them, just like you needed."

I laughed again at his enthusiasm. "Your Grandpa Clemens would be proud of your good counsel." A pang of grief plucked at my stomach.

Nathaniel scribbled my twelve points onto the scorecard.

"Nathaniel, you know, your great Grandpa Clemens was a minister. One of the things he did best was visiting people and making them feel wanted and comfortable in the church. He used to joke that he never went anywhere without his guitar, his dice, and his cards."

Nathaniel lifted his eyebrows as if to ask what was so funny about that.

"People used to think that playing with cards and dice was like gambling, which is a big 'no, no' in the church. And the guitar, well that was an instrument musicians played in bars, which also would be looked down on in the church. But Grandpa used his guitar to sing Christian hymns and choruses. He had a beautiful bass voice. And the dice and cards were his Yahtzee dice and his Rook cards. He carried them so he could have fun with folks. That's always a good way to build relationships."

"Grandpa Clemens played Rook?" Nathaniel's voice rose in excitement. Rook was his most recently acquired game, and now his favorite.

"Oh yes. You know, that's where I learned Rook. He taught Mamaw, and Mamaw taught me, and I taught you. I think Grandpa Clemens was probably one of the best Rook players around. He loved to play. At holidays when we all got together we used to play and play. I have many fond memories of sitting around the card table, eating cold turkey sandwiches and playing Rook with Grandpa."

I sighed. Grandpa had suffered several years with Parkinson's and dementia before he died. "You never really knew him before he got sick. I wish you could have known him then. He would have loved playing games with you."

The miles of asphalt droned beneath us as I sat in somber reflection. Nathaniel tapped the die roller against his leg and looked out the window. "Mama, maybe someday I'll get to play Rook with Grandpa in heaven."

Tears of grief and joy stung my eyes.

"Yes, son. I know Grandpa would like that. . . . Hey, kiddo, it's your turn."

Reflections

Because of Jesus Christ's finished work defeating death, in *him* we have continuity between generations, a rich and full heritage. As Christians we need to grieve the loss of those we love when they die, but we need not grieve as those who have no hope of seeing their loved ones again. We treasure the wisdom and the witness of those in our Christian family who have come and gone before us, knowing that they are alive and well with our Father in heaven.

Prayer

Dear God, some whom I have loved have left their earthly bodies and gone ahead of me into heaven. When I remember them, help me to have the simple faith of a child. Help me to grieve as one who has hope in you and assurance of eternal life in Christ. Thank you for the marvelous mystery, that through past ages and the ages to come we are one family in you. Amen.

DRESSING UP FOR GOD

*Dear friends, now we are children of God, and what we
will be has not yet been made known. But we know
that when he appears, we shall be like him, for we shall
see him as he is.*

—1 John 3:2

CHRISTIANA AND Hannah scooted into the kitchen and stood by the bench where I was working. Christiana half hid behind Hannah and gave her a little push. I studied my daughters, now three and five years old, waiting to hear about what they wanted but didn't want to ask.

Hannah finally spoke. "Mommy, can we dress up?"

"Sure." Why had they asked special permission? The basket of dress-up clothes in their bedroom was always available. They didn't dart away. "And . . . ?"

Hannah giggled. "Could we use makeup?"

"Oh, I see. Well, that's a different thing altogether."

"Pleeeze!" Christiana and Hannah chorused. I think they had been practicing—very hard to resist.

"You two. Let me think for a minute."

Where was that makeup? I'd received a kit from a friend a couple of years earlier but had never used it. The large compact was a collection of multicolor powders, eye shadows, and blushes.

"All right, girls. Follow me." I pulled the compact out of the bathroom closet and set it on the counter. The case was about five-by-seven inches, trimmed in gold. Christiana's and Hannah's eyes grew wide.

"Now, these are the eye shadows, and these are the blushes for your cheeks, and here is even a lipstick. Try not to get too messy, OK?"

They nodded.

"Have fun. I'll be in the kitchen if you need me."

Two minutes later, Hannah appeared in the doorway of the kitchen clothed in a faded and discarded pajama top with her frilly slip over the top.

"You look lovely."

"Mommy, could we use your hair stuff?"

I pondered for a minute.

"Pleeeze?"

What could it hurt?

"All right. Just be careful with them."

"Thanks, Mommy!" she called as she skipped away.

Hannah was back in a moment with my largest, fluffiest hair bow, a bright multicolored pink. "Can you do this for me?"

Hannah's red curls fought me as I gathered them up.

"Do you want it in back?"

"Up here." She placed her hand on top of her head.

I dropped the back layer of curls and herded the stray wisps upward, then I snapped the bow on. It was almost too big for me to wear, and on Hannah's head—the top of Hannah's head—it made her look like Pebbles Flintstone. I suppressed a laugh. "You take a look and see if that's what you had in mind."

As I worked in the kitchen, the exclamations and giggles from the bathroom down the hall entertained me. Then the giggles drew near and the big moment arrived. What a sight!

Hannah had kept her bright pink bow atop her red curls. Her face was caked in myriad colors, the layers blotched on the cheeks and eyes. Her nose was powdered a dominant blue with traces of pink and purple. The tip of her nose was powdered so thickly that no sign of her freckles peeked through. Around her lips—not a bit on the lips—she'd traced a line of red lipstick. In a final touch of artistry she'd draped several strands of purple and pink plastic beads down her front.

Christiana was dressed in an outgrown blue-striped, white pajama jumpsuit, sporting a clownish ruffle around the neck. On her head was my black felt bowler with velveteen ribbon bow. Like Hannah, Christiana's smiling face appeared to have suffered a run-in with an artist's pallet (although not nearly as striking as Hannah's).

"Wow! You guys are really something! Are you gorgeous or what?"

The girls giggled. Hannah asked, "Can we show Daddy when he gets home?"

"Oh, absolutely. I know he wouldn't want to miss this."

Christiana stood tall and tilted her head in perfect model fashion. "Mommy, do you really think we're pretty?"

"Of course. You're always beautiful."

"Then can we dress up like this and wear your makeup to church Sunday?"

Reflections

The Christian life is a growing process. We begin our spiritual life saved but not perfected, not completely like God in the beauty of love and wisdom, peace, goodness, kindness, self-control, joy, and faithfulness. Sometimes we find it difficult to be satisfied with our growth process. But, if we "try on" these out-workings of the Spirit in sizes that are not yet fitting for us, it doesn't help us grow faster or be more mature. In fact, we might appear to be awkward or even hypocritical! We need to focus on our relationship with our heavenly parent, who is the source of our growing and gifting.

Prayer

Dear God, I like to dress up for you, to try wearing your goodness, decorating myself with your joy and peace, showing off your wisdom. But what is awesome and beautiful on you, sometimes looks overdone or ostentatious on me. I know it pleases you that I want to be like you. Help me to be patient with letting those outward signs of knowing you increase and manifest naturally, as fitting expressions of growing up into your image. Thank you for loving me as your precious, beautiful child, no matter how I'm dressed! Amen.

POISON SOUP

Our fathers disciplined us for a little while as they thought best; but God disciplines us for our good, that we may share in his holiness. No discipline seems pleasant at the time, but painful. Later on, however, it produces a harvest of righteousness and peace for those who have been trained by it.

—Hebrews 12:10–11

"MOMMY, CAN WE HAVE some bowls?" Hannah asked. "We're making soup."

I glanced at my four-year-old—her red curls were knotted and her cheeks smudged with mud. She looked like a poster child for Lazy Summer Play Days.

"Sure, honey. Take a couple of the butter dishes from the bottom cabinet next to the garage door." I pointed.

"Thanks, Mom." Hannah snatched two bowls and dashed out the door.

I went back to sorting and clearing the papers off my kitchen catch-all counter.

Fifteen minutes later I finally got down to the countertop as I placed an old church bulletin in the to-be-trashed pile and one of Nathaniel's school papers in the to-be-filed stack.

Hannah flung open the door and edged into the kitchen, still holding onto the door knob. Her gaze darted around the kitchen and she shifted her weight from foot to foot.

"Is something wrong? Do you need to go potty?"

"No, it's not that . . ."

I waited.

Hannah chewed her lower lip. "Christiana got some stuff out of the garage to put in the soup and she spilled some."

"Oh?" I crossed the kitchen as I spoke, anxiety tickling my stomach. "What kind of stuff?" I turned Hannah toward the garage and urged her ahead of me. She strode into the garage through the obstacle course of bicycles and lawn care equipment toward the utility shelves in the back. She pointed to a heavy plastic container lying on its side next to a puddle of viscous blue liquid. Antifreeze!

An article I'd read flashed through my mind—on the fatal consequences of antifreeze to dogs. The article said that the poisonous substance had a mildly sweet flavor dogs liked . . . and children too? Especially a child who experienced her world through tactile, hands-on involvement? The anxious tickle in my stomach exploded into an adrenaline rush constricting my throat and quickening my pulse.

"You didn't eat any of that soup, did you, Hannah?"

Hannah's eyes widened. She stepped away responding to the intensity of my voice. "I didn't!"

"Did Christiana?"

"I don't know." Tears filled Hannah's eyes. The puppy trotted into the garage, tail wagging in ignorant bliss. I grabbed her collar.

"Hannah, take Sophie and *don't* let her get near this antifreeze."

Hannah hesitated.

I shoved the dog in her direction. "Take her!"

Hannah's anxiety burst into sobs as she hugged the dog. "I told her not to . . ."

I lost the rest of Hannah's lament as I dashed out the back door to find Christiana, that naughty—wonderful—child I loved. I sighted her—she was bent over butter dishes and sand buckets, stirring and talking.

"Christiana!"

I ran toward her. Christiana turned from her concoction and looked in my direction. I squinted my eyes, looking around her mouth for any evidence that she had sampled her soup.

"Christiana," I panted as I knelt next to her and grabbed her shoulders, "did you eat any of the soup?"

Christiana's eyes were wide, her mouth open. She shook her head. "Are you sure?" I inadvertently punctuated each word with a squeeze. She pulled away, trying to free herself from my grasp. "I didn't!"

Tears filled my eyes. I grabbed her and hugged her; the panic drained away.

Now I held her at arm's length, fury replacing my fear.

"Christiana, don't you *ever* touch anything of Mama's or Papa's in the garage again! Do you hear me?"

"I didn't—"

"Yes, you did!"

Christiana's jaw tightened. She pulled away and crossed her arms. "But I needed it."

"Christiana, it could have killed you, or Hannah, or Sophie! It's poisonous!"

Christiana only narrowed her eyes at me. Her defensive posture and self-justification blocked any light of understanding or repentance.

I lowered my voice. "Some things are poisonous. That means that they can hurt you. They can make you very, very sick—or even kill you—if you eat them or drink them."

Christiana looked down and kicked at her soup bowls.

"Christiana, I love you and I don't want you to get hurt. You'll have to take a time-out for climbing the shelves and getting into the anti-freeze. And we *must* throw *this* soup away and wash out the dishes."

"Th'ow out my soup?" She glared.

My explanation and my affection paled when pitted against the product of her morning's creative effort.

I sighed my frustration away and rubbed her back. "How about if I help you and Hannah make some good soup later in the kitchen?"

Christiana weighed my offer then acted her consent by nudging closer.

I pulled her near for a reconciliatory hug, thankful for once that she was a picky eater.

Reflections

We are God's children with limited understanding of all the whys of God's life-giving, life-preserving guidelines for our lives. Since the beginning of the world, God as our heavenly parent has loved us deeply, and has lamented our stubborn and disobedient bent toward eternal self-destruction. Perhaps God's anger is similar to our anger with our children when they disobey and act foolishly, endangering themselves and others.

Prayer

Dear loving God, when I fear your awesome anger as recorded in Scripture, I struggle sometimes to feel safe with you and simply trust your love for me. Help me to trust that your commandments and your guidance are for my safety and eternal well-being. Help me have faith that your anger is not bent on my destruction but is forever seated in your love. Amen.

Day 11

THAT'S WHAT MOMMIES ARE FOR

The LORD is faithful to all his promises
and loving toward all he has made.
The LORD upholds all those who fall
and lifts up all who are bowed down.

—Psalm 145:13–14

Are not two sparrows sold for a penny? Yet not one of
them will fall to the ground apart from the will of your
Father. And even the very hairs of your head are all
numbered. So don't be afraid; you are worth more than
many sparrows.

—Matthew 10:29–31

I GRASPED CHRISTIANA'S ankles and pulled her up . . . up . . . up in her swing and then let go.

She laughed.

I stepped away as she swooshed back toward me.

Hannah whined, "My turn."

"Not right now, Hannah. I've been pushing you girls for twenty minutes. I have some work I want to get done in the garden. Aren't ya'll getting tired of swinging?"

"No!" both girls answered.

"It's no fun if you're not pushing us," said Hannah.

"Then you'll have to find something else to do."

52

Christiana skidded to a stop. "Can we ride bikes?"

I paused. We lived on a fairly busy street, and the girls were both just getting off of training wheels. I still liked to be nearby, observing, when they were riding. But it was something else for them to do, and promised me a little time to work on the herb bed I was trying to prepare before the summer was too far gone. We did have a double driveway and if . . .

"I tell you what. How about if I park the van across the end of the driveway to get it out of your way and to keep you from accidentally going out into the street?"

"Sure!"

Hannah was off her swing headed for the garage with Christiana close behind.

Thirty minutes later I wiggled an unwieldy landscaping timber into place, then headed to the garage for the steel rods that would hold the beams in place.

A wail of agony floated over the roof from the front of the house. I ran toward the side gate and Hannah met me halfway.

"Mama, Christiana's hurt."

I bypassed Hannah and hurried to Christiana's side.

When she saw me her whimpers exploded into a piteous wail. "Mommy! Mommy! I can't—"

Christiana lay partly under and partly on top of the pink and purple frame of her bicycle. The toe of her top foot was twisted and pinned between the chain and the pedal. The pedal beneath was pinned against the concrete by Christiana's weight.

"Oh dear. It's all right, honey, let me see."

I carefully lifted the bike frame and hoisted Christiana up off the concrete. After an extended hug, a few tears, and three bandages, Christiana and Hannah were off and riding again, and I was back filling my herb bed with topsoil and manure.

The rest of the afternoon and evening were pleasant and

uneventful. Our summer day ended with supper time, bath time, and bedtime.

I tucked Hannah into her bed and walked across the hall to Christiana's room. She was already snuggled under her covers in her top bunk—an unusual occurrence without parental encouragement.

I stepped on the lower bunk, wiggling my foot between a stuffed Barney and a doll bed, and pulled myself to eye level with Christiana. Christiana grabbed me around the neck and gave me a quick hug. I laughed and grasped the top rail to keep from losing my balance.

"Mommy, you picked me up," Christiana said. Her tone was one of revelation, a conclusion reached after intense reflection.

Christiana often uttered phrases out of context, and I was used to decoding them. I searched back through the events of the day.

"Oh, you mean when you fell on your bike. Yes, sweetheart, of course."

"That's what mommies are for, to help you up when you fall."

"Yes, that's what mommies are for."

Reflections

Sometimes when we fall down or fail in our lives we feel like God will be angry or displeased, and we are ashamed to go to him. But when Jesus bore our sins and infirmities on the cross, he also freed us of the shame and guilt of failure and falling.

God, our heavenly Father, knows that when we come to him we've already been hurt in our hearts and souls, we've experienced the painful consequences of falling down. If we are proud and in denial of our faults and failings, God may reprimand us as a good parent would. But when we—hurting and humbled—confess our fall, God rescues us. As our heavenly parent, he picks us up and comforts us in *his* loving arms. God will tenderly wipe away our tears, patch up our hurts, and encourage us to ride again.

Prayer

Dear God, you know my heart; you know when I'm avoiding you, hiding my failures and my injured pride. You know when I'm hurting and humbled and ready to receive the comfort and encouragement you wait to give me. I'm your growing child with so much to learn. With you as my heavenly parent, I can venture on, because I know that you will always be there for me with able, loving arms to lift me up and steady me when I fall. Thank you! In Jesus' name, Amen.

$\mathcal{A}$ LEGO GARDEN

He also said, "This is what the kingdom of God is like. A man scatters seed on the ground. Night and day, whether he sleeps or gets up, the seed sprouts and grows, though he does not know how. All by itself the soil produces grain—first the stalk, then the head, then the full kernel in the head. As soon as the grain is ripe, he puts the sickle to it, because the harvest has come."

—Mark 4:26–29

Let us not become weary in doing good, for at the proper time we will reap a harvest if we do not give up.

—Galatians 6:9

BETWEEN THE AGES OF six and ten Nathaniel used every birthday and Christmas dollar, every hard-earned buck, to build his treasured Lego collection. Nathaniel was generally a giving little boy; in the *Revised Nathaniel Version* of the Bible, however, sharing did not apply to Lego tiles and figures. I occasionally required him to let his sisters or other little visitors play with his Lego collection, but his impatience and his insistence on dictating terms discouraged creative play. So the girls asked less and less.

After several lectures urging him to soften his stance in the name of the Golden Rule, I sighed and resigned myself to years of domestic conflict on behalf of these tiny, bottle-headed, plastic beings. *Another lesson lost, role models forgotten, words unheard.* When it came to his Lego collection, I was certain that the seeds I'd tried to sow—love and sharing and valuing people over things—had died without germination.

Long after I had settled for an uneasy truce concerning Nathaniel's Legos, I passed his bedroom one afternoon and heard him talking. I yielded to the mom's right to eavesdrop, since it was Christiana, not Nathaniel, who usually talked to herself while playing.

Nathaniel's voice reflected the gentle authority of a teacher, instructing, yes, but not commanding. "Here, Hannah, you take the big castle and these guys and horses so that you'll be the safest. And, Christiana, you take this castle and these boats. I'll put my guys here on this island with these boats. You two have the castles, so that will make things fair."

I crept to the doorway for a peek, to see if this happy play scene between the siblings was reality or wishful thinking.

Hannah gathered her appointed pile of plastic soldiers together and began placing them along the walls of her gray and black block castle. Christiana lined up the half dozen boats along the shore of her white, blue, yellow, and red edifice.

Christiana looked up. "Hi, Mommy. We're playing castles. I got lots of treasure." She held aloft a tiny brown treasure chest and flipped open the lid to reveal dozens of miniature, golden plastic discs.

"Yes, I can see that. Very nice, Nathaniel."

Nathaniel shrugged. His hands darted back and forth amid a pile of blocks, weapons, and people parts, all varying sizes and shapes. He was creating a makeshift fortress, and snapping together an assortment of pirates, island natives, and outer-space warriors. His confident dexterity was that of one who'd spent hundreds of hours at this creative endeavor.

Hannah held up two thumb-height knights astride their sturdy mounts, complete with form-fitted armor, capes, tack, and matching coat-of-arms banners. "Look what Nathaniel gave me to play with."

"Wow! Looks like you have a fighting chance to protect your treasure with all that neat stuff."

Nathaniel glanced up with the sly grin of a master strategist. "Don't bet on it. I've got some pretty mean dudes here, and we're ready to go get treasure."

"Remember, it's supposed to be fun."

Nathaniel gave me a cursory nod.

I left the doorway, experiencing a moment of content at this remarkable accomplishment. Everyone was happy. Everyone was sharing. A sprig had sprouted and a bud of benevolence had blossomed when I wasn't looking. I called Don to report the unimaginable moment.

But why was I surprised? We'd planted seeds of caring, and worked hard to water, weed, and provide fertile soil on many a weary day. After that wondrous afternoon, Nathaniel still had conflict with his sisters about Lego logistics, but the glimpse of growth I saw that day let me know that, when I plant the seeds of truth and charity, God is faithful to steadily grow gardens of love in my children's hearts.

Reflections

Our responsibility as parents is to love our children, to teach our children the truth, to discipline them when they need directing, to daily lift them before God in prayer. We can require loving and kind outward behavior but we cannot make our children love others or God. Our children are people created in the image of God with free will to choose their attitudes and behaviors. We plant seeds and tend the garden, but God must bring the growth.

We as God's children grow in the same way; God plants seeds in our hearts, through his Word, through the examples of other believers, through books we read or speakers to whom we listen. We need to carefully tend the gardens of our souls, but then, as always, inner growth and blossoms of love in our child hearts will require the miraculous work of God's Holy Spirit.

Prayer

Dear God, I must plant seeds and then water and weed my flowers so they may flourish. In the same way, help me to faithfully nurture, teach, and discipline my children and my own soul so that our tender hearts may grow in your loving ways. Give me patience when the job seems endless and unfruitful. Help me cherish the blossoms bursting forth in my children and in myself, and to celebrate the beauty of your creation in each of us just as you do. Amen.

GOD THE TEACHER

*Take my yoke upon you and learn from me, for I am
gentle and humble in heart, and you will find rest for
your souls. For my yoke is easy and my burden is light.*
—Matthew 11:29–30

*I will instruct you and teach you in the way
    you should go;
I will counsel you and watch over you.*
—Psalm 32:8

I SAT ON THE STOOP, looking through junk mail and waiting
for Hannah's school bus to arrive. The driver wouldn't let kindergart-
ners off unless a parent was visibly present—a good policy that provided for child safety. It also provided a few unstructured moments
for waiting parents. The school bus rumbled up the street, cueing me
to toss the empty envelopes and sales brochures into the outdoor trash.

As I walked toward the road, the groaning yellow-orange giant rolled
up. The squeal of the brakes and sigh of the opening doors announced
the arrival of my younger daughter, who had completed her first week
of "big" school. Hannah's lunch box banged against her side, drum-
ming the after-school rattle as she bounded across the road and into
the driveway.

"Hi, Hannah. How was your day?"

"Good." She set her lunch box down in the middle of the driveway
and swung her Winnie-the-Pooh backpack off her shoulder.

I put my arm around her shoulders and gave her a quick side hug. "Do you have something to show me?"

Hannah unzipped her bag and pulled out a crumpled Crayola-covered paper. An alligator, an apple, an astronaut, and an ant surrounded the outlined letter "Aa."

"Very nice!"

"I made a friend." Her gray-green eyes shone. "Her name is Amanda and she sat with me at lunch. And I didn't get my name on the board any this week." (Hannah had informed me the first day of school that children who did not follow the rules had their names written on the board.) Hannah pulled on the "A" paper in my hand. "Tomorrow Teacher says we're going to start on 'B.'"

"Tomorrow's Saturday, Hannah. You don't go to school tomorrow."

She gazed down at her "A" paper and her voice dropped. "Oh."

"Would you like a snack?"

"No."

"How about a drink?"

"OK."

We walked into the house and Hannah plopped down on the bench in our kitchen. She leaned back, swinging her feet, and gazed past me to some point above the refrigerator.

I handed her a glass of lemonade and stroked back the red curls that had escaped her ponytail holder. Then I sat down across the table from her, waiting for further news of her school day. Hannah sipped her drink and studied a tiny tear in the vinyl tablecloth.

As she reached out to pick at the damaged patch, I deflected her hand. "Please don't."

She sat back—without her usual defense to my reprimand—and heaved a short sigh. "I wish I could go to school every day."

I smiled. *I wonder how long this will last.* "That's neat. I'm glad you like school so much."

She sat in silence for a moment. "Will I always get to go to school?"

"You'll be in school a long time. Some people choose to keep going to school most of their lives. At any rate, you don't ever have to stop learning."

Hannah sipped her drink. She wrinkled her forehead, usually a prelude to her next question.

"Is there going to be school in heaven?" she asked.

"Hmm." I sat back in the bench and pondered for a moment. "That's a good question. Maybe so. I suppose we'll still have things to learn in heaven."

Hannah gulped the last swallow of lemonade with the gusto of a kindergartner who has resolved yet another mystery of life. "Then in heaven, God will be the teacher."

Reflections

God, through the ministry of Jesus Christ and the Holy Spirit, fulfills the roll of our greatest teacher. We are his students, young children with so much to learn! We often measure our success in terms of action and production. But Jesus emphasized the inner life and our attitudes as the essential starting point of all spiritual learning that leads to transformation of outward action.

Prayer

Dear God, I like to think that for all eternity we will be learning lessons of love from you. As I grow in and toward eternal reality, help me to develop the attributes of a good learner. May I listen more and talk less, pay attention to the teacher instead of copying off my neighbor's paper, and may I daily enter the school of eternal life with the enthusiasm and wonder of a young child. Amen.

*L*OSING GOD

*For I am convinced that neither death nor life, neither
angels nor demons, neither the present nor the future,
nor any powers, neither height nor depth, nor anything
else in all creation, will be able to separate us from the
love of God that is in Christ Jesus our Lord.*

—Romans 8:38–39

MY ATTENTION SHIFTED from the magazine article in front of me to the sound of feet stomping up the stairs. The kitchen door flew open and Nathaniel stormed passed me. His eyebrows were knit down to his nose and he glared straight ahead.

"Christiana, have you been in my room?!" He covered the distance between his basement bedroom and Christiana's room, impelled by the fervor of righteous wrath.

I lay my magazine on the table and followed, in case I was needed to referee. I could hear Christiana talking to her imaginary class. Her voice lilted with the tone of praise and encouragement for a job well done.

Nathaniel stopped at Christiana's bedroom door. His breathing was accentuated by an edge of physical and emotional exertion.

"Did you get into my Legos?"

Christiana stopped playing and looked up, startled and apprehensive. "No."

I thought her denial might need bolstering by an alibi. "She's been upstairs all morning."

"I'm trying to build a space cruiser and I can't find all the pieces.

They were there when I made it before. Are you sure you didn't take anything?"

Christiana threw onto the bed the school papers she was holding and grabbed the door. "Brother, I did not take it!" She began to push the door shut.

I stepped in front of Nathaniel and caught the door with my hand. "Don't slam doors, Christiana; it's dangerous." I turned to Nathaniel. "I don't think she did it. You have so many pieces scattered all over the floor. I'd think it would be easy to lose a particular piece. Are you sure it's missing, or is it just misplaced?"

"Yeah . . . I think so."

"Isn't there another piece that you could use?"

"No. Not to make this ship."

"Why don't you look again."

Nathaniel slumped his shoulders and reluctantly complied.

"Do you need any help?" Christiana asked.

"No." Nathaniel shuffled through the house on his way back downstairs.

I smiled at Christiana. "That was nice of you to offer to help brother. I don't think he's in the mood for help right now. Sometimes people feel sort of angry with themselves when they lose something that's important to them; sometimes they take out their frustration on anyone who's around. It's better to just leave him alone for a while."

"I don't lose stuff."

I looked at the clutter in Christiana's room. Dozens of graded and returned school papers and outfits of clothes lay in piles, scattered around the room. They represented Christiana's imaginary students and their work. Her dolls and stuffed animals were gathered together in a box at the foot of her bed. But what she *really* cared about were her fanciful students. She was right. It's hard to lose invisible friends.

Reflections

God understands that it's hard to let go of people and things we care about. But God wishes for us to be free of the anxiety of losing. Through Christ, God has made an incredible promise that we need never be separated from that which is most important—God, God's love, God's family.

Lifting those things we are afraid of losing into the care of God can help us keep this eternal perspective in the center of our lives. So that wherever we go and whatever we do throughout our day, we can be at peace in the assurance of this promise.

Prayer

Dear God, I'm sometimes afraid of losing. I worry about losing my job, my stuff, my relationships, even my beliefs. I'm often anxious because I'm trying to hold on to things that will someday pass away. Help me spend my time and energy pursuing the things that are eternal—the invisible realities of your kingdom. Your love, your Word, your guidance, your presence, your joy, and your peace are things I can never lose. When I seek you, you are near me. Because you have promised never to leave me, I can rest in the blessed hope and truth that I never can lose you. Amen.

THE PRODIGAL PARENT

*If you, then, though you are evil, know how to give good
gifts to your children, how much more will your Father
in heaven give good gifts to those who ask him!*

—Matthew 7:11

*And so we know and rely on the love God has for us.
God is love.*

—1 John 4:16

Though he slay me, yet will I hope in him.

—Job 13:15

ON A PEG IN THE entry space between the back door and the
kitchen door, hung the blue, dirty-feet towel. Since the previous night's
thunderstorms had replenished the backyard mud supply, the towel
was more brown than blue and more wet than dry. Our beagle, Sophie,
whined to be let inside, out of the marshland.

I opened the door and she trotted in.

"Sit!"

Sophie obeyed. Sophie was no exception when it came to obeying
Mom's first commandment: Thou shalt not enter the house until thy
filthy feet have been thoroughly wiped.

I pulled the towel from its peg and worked Sophie's paws over with
the vigor of a white tornado. I was determined that my new beige
berber carpet would not wear the hues of the rainy season. I gave my
dog her release command and she bolted for her food dish.

From the swing set, I heard Christiana and Hannah singing. I stood in the doorway and observed their rhythmic flight over the puddles that had collected beneath the swings. A reminder of Mom's first commandment wouldn't hurt.

"Remember, girls, when you come in, please wipe off your feet!"

Hannah called back. "Yes, Mama." The singsong in her voice implied that I had told her this a million times and, of course, she would remember.

"Christiana? You'll remember to wipe your feet, right?"

Christiana squinted in my direction, indicating that she was making an effort to shift her attention from her world of swinging. "OK." Her voice held the semiconscious conviction of someone waking from a dream. But I knew that she knew the rule—everyone in our house knew the rule.

I glanced at the clock on my computer. I'd been working for almost two hours without interruption. I guess the mud had one advantage— its appeal for outdoor play. Now it was time to start supper.

When I came upstairs, past the back entryway, my feelings of contentment over the afternoon's accomplishments drained away. Both the back door and kitchen door stood open. The foot towel hung happily on its peg. Brownish-black foot-shaped blotches led from the door, through the kitchen, down the berber carpet in the hallway, and into the bathroom.

Dinner would be late.

I stomped down the hallway, cringing at every dark splotch that marred my carpet. I pounded on the bathroom door.

"Christiana, you forgot to wipe your feet!"

"I had to go to the bathroom, quick."

The door opened and Christiana started out into the hallway. I stepped in front of her, blocking her way back onto the carpet. "You have *got* to remember to wipe your feet. Next time come in sooner so you have time."

"OK, Mommy."

She spoke in the same noncommittal tone she'd used earlier from the swing set. This was the third time this week she'd tracked mud into the house.

A wave of frustration rushed up, pouring out in a torrent.

"No, it is *not* OK. You have *got* to listen to me. This has *got* to stop!"

Christiana adopted her defensive posture, her eyes narrowing into slits. "It's not fair!"

"What is 'not fair' is that you are ruining my carpet! You will wash your feet, change your clothes, and sit on the couch until dinner!"

Christiana's squinty eyes widened and filled with tears. I realized that my voice had continued to rise until my last tirade was an all-out yell. I sighed and shook my head as much at myself as at my careless daughter.

"I'll run your bath and get you a change of clothes."

I adjusted the water temperature from cold to hot to warm, softening under the conviction of Christiana's sniffles.

Sitting on the couch until dinner was a long stretch for Christiana. I flipped the hamburgers and sauntered into the living room. Christiana, feeling misunderstood and dejected, rolled away from me to hide her face against the couch cushions.

I sat on the edge of the couch. "Christiana . . ."

No response.

"Christiana, you *do* need to obey Mommy and remember to clean your feet when you come inside. But Mommy should not have yelled at you so loud. I'm sorry. Will you forgive me?"

Christiana rolled over and nodded.

"Thank you."

Christiana's face popped into a smile and she sprang into my arms. "No matter what you do to me, you still love me!"

"Yes, Christiana. I always still love you."

Reflections

Sometimes we have trouble believing that God truly loves us. But how do we define God's love for us? Does God's loving us mean that he gives us everything we want and promises us no hardships? Of course not. Or does God's loving us mean that he uses everthing that happens in our lives to draw us closer to him? Yes! Thinking of our imperfect yet enduring love for our children can help us to have faith in God's perfect love as an unshakable fact, no matter what our circumstances.

Prayer

Dear God, I am such an imperfect parent! And yet, even when I make mistakes and exhibit unloving ways, my daughter knows that I love her. You are my perfect heavenly father and mother, perfect in love and grace. From your perspective of eternity, you always know what is best for me. You love me so much more than any earthly parent could. When the circumstances in my life are hard to deal with and seem unfair, help me to be a trusting child, keeping my faith fixed on your love in every circumstance. Amen.

WHEN I WANT TO

Do not merely listen to the word, and so deceive yourselves. Do what it says. Anyone who listens to the word but does not do what it says is like a man who looks at his face in a mirror and, after looking at himself, goes away and immediately forgets what he looks like. But the man who looks intently into the perfect law that gives freedom, and continues to do this, not forgetting what he has heard, but doing it—he will be blessed in what he does.

—James 1:22–25

If anyone obeys his word, God's love is truly made complete in him.

—1 John 2:5

Whatever you do, work at it with all your heart, as working for the Lord, not for men, since you know that you will receive an inheritance from the Lord as a reward. It is the Lord Christ you are serving.

—Colossians 3:23–24

"HI, MOM." HANNAH'S greeting ended in a gloomy sigh. She climbed onto the bench in the kitchen and hoisted herself onto the window ledge to watch me wash the dishes.

"What's the matter, Hannah?"

"I'm bored."

I tried to remember when I last had time to be bored. I smiled at my inability to recall any such moment since I had been blessed with children.

Hannah's brow furrowed into a scowl. "Are you laughing at me?"

"No. I'm not laughing at you. I was smiling because I can't remember the last time I was bored. How about playing with your dolls or writing a letter to Grandma?"

"No. Not right now." Hannah looked up, following the path of a tiny spider as it darted across the ceiling.

"I'm sure you can find something to do."

My despondent daughter frowned and slid from the windowsill to the bench.

I tried again. "What's Christiana up to?"

Hannah bounced twice on the bench before springing to an Olympic two-point landing on the floor. "She's playing with her papers. She doesn't want to play with me."

"I see."

Hannah sauntered over to me and leaned her head on my side. "I want to do something with you."

I moved Hannah back a few inches with my arm as I put the last plate in the dishwasher. She grabbed my arm and pulled at me.

"Oh, sweetie, I'd love to do something with you, but I need to finish up here and get those flowers into the ground this afternoon. I bought them two days ago and they need to be planted."

Hannah let go of my arm. I poured the dish detergent in the waiting cups and shut the door.

"Why is it that you always have work to do but I get bored?"

I wiped my hands on a towel. "That's a good question. You have work to do also, but I guess not as much."

"I know. I'll help Mommy!" Hannah's eyes brightened and she bounced on her toes.

"That's a terrific idea. Let's see . . . you could wipe off the dining room table for me."

Hannah stopped bouncing. "Is there something else?"

"OK. How about if you clean the fronts of the kitchen cabinets. They really need it."

Hannah looked down at the floor. Her smile twisted in distaste.

"I thought you liked washing the cabinets," I said.

"But I've done that before. How about something else? Can I mop the floor?"

"Hannah, you tried to mop not long ago. You're not quite strong enough to do that job, remember?"

"All right. How about if I help you plant the flowers?"

"That would be great, but we have to pull the weeds out of the flower bed first. I'd love for you to help me with that."

Hannah looked past me to the sunny world out the window and hesitated. I knew from past experience that weeding the flower bed was not her idea of a good time.

"Hannah, you asked if you could help me, and weeding is one way you can be with me. But you don't want to do the things that need to be done."

"I know, but . . ."

How had I gotten myself into the unenviable position of chairing the draft board?

"Look—how about if you wipe off the table? Then I'll call for you when I finish weeding, and you can help me plant the begonias."

Hannah nodded and smiled. I imagined her pleasure was not so much from helping me out as from relief that I hadn't insisted she work at something she didn't like.

"OK." Cured of her boredom, Hannah snatched the wet dishcloth from the sink and headed for the dining room.

Reflections

Often we think of doing God's work in terms of actions that are focused on church activities. And at times God does call us to use our gifts in church programs. But when considering the work God is asking us to do, we also need to listen to the prompting of the Spirit, who might be asking us to work inside our daily relationships, in our homes, or even in our hearts.

When responding to requests from people to do a certain work for God, we sometimes feel trapped and overburdened. But when we are seeking God's direction, James exhorts us not to look to other people but to look instead into the "perfect law *that gives freedom*." Then, in doing what we find in God's perfect law, we will be blessed, not burdened.

Prayer

Dear God, how often I ask you to show me the work that you want me to do, only to draw back from the reality of your requests. The idea of serving you is exciting and full of warm feelings of love. Day-to-day obedience to your call is sometimes tedious and difficult, so sometimes I ask you to give me an exiting new job, or a more important job, or a fun job that produces immediate results. Help me to be content with the work you give me. Help me to know that whatever work you give is part of your plan to bless me and to produce everlasting results among your family. Amen.

$\mathcal{J}$F GOD MEANT FOR US TO FLY, HE WOULD HAVE GIVEN US SWINGS

This is the day the LORD has made;
let us rejoice and be glad in it.

—Psalm 118:24

Rejoice in the Lord always. I will say it again: Rejoice!
—Philippians 4:4

I have come that they may have life, and have it to the
full.

—John 10:10

"CAN I GO OUT AND SWING?"

"*May* I go out and swing? Have you brushed your teeth, Christiana? Are you all ready for school?"

"Yes."

I glanced at the clock. Twenty minutes until bus time. I'd never heard of any kid like her. Most days Christiana got ready for school early in order to go out and swing.

"OK. I'll call you in when it's time to go."

Christiana scampered out the back door and I continued packing lunches.

Nathaniel and Hannah sat at the kitchen table eating cereal.

Don joined us. "Where's Christiana?"

"Swinging," answered Hannah.

"Figures." He smiled at me and shook his head. "I wonder why she likes to swing so much?"

I zipped up Nathaniel's lunch bag and handed it to him. "Maybe she just likes the way it feels."

"But she doesn't *do* anything," Nathaniel said.

I placed the other two lunch boxes on the table and went to the sink to wash my hands. "That's all right. It's good exercise, and she enjoys it."

"I like to swing, too." Hannah said.

"Yeah," said Nathaniel, "but you don't get up early in the morning to do it."

Now it was Hannah's turn to shake her head and roll her eyes.

"Knock it off, you two," said Don.

I walked into the living room to watch Christiana from the window. She swung forward as far as the chains would allow, lifting off the seat slightly before swinging back, swooping over the ground and flying up to brush her head against the leaves that hung behind the swing set. As she swung, I could see her singing to herself. Her eyes seemed focused on another place, and a smile lit up her face.

After school, I took the children to the park. They ran to the newly constructed play area, a colorful maze of connected ramps and swinging bridges, slides, and ladders. I lagged behind and made my way through the abandoned, older area of the playground. The weatherworn wooden seesaws and the old belt-style swings looked lonesome. I settled into one of the swings. How many years had it been? I kicked off to get a good start and then pumped my legs back and forth in rhythm, tucking my feet under so as not to scrape the ground.

On the forward movement, the air rushed past my face, pulling my hair behind me, and then into my face as I swung back. I gained height, stretching my toes up toward the blue canopy and hanging for that glorious, weightless moment before plunging backward toward the ground. The tingle in my stomach as I swooped back and forth took me to other playgrounds and the joy of the unhindered motion and rhythm of swinging.

"Hey, Mom, what are you doing?" Nathaniel's incredulous shout broke into my yesteryears.

I stopped pumping and coasted to a gentle sway. "Swinging. Just swinging."

Reflections

Certain simple activities or situations can bring us happiness and contentment. Often, thinking back to our childhoods can conjure a wistful memory. In this world God has created, he has provided a myriad of smells, sights, sounds, textures, and tastes. It pleases God for his children to play in this wonderful playground of creation.

Prayer

Dear God, remind me of the joy of living, of the simple pleasures you have given me in your bountiful creation. Help me to realize that accomplishing tasks that produce a product is only part of your plan. Help me to take notice of the senses you have created in me, and to experience the genuine enjoyment they can bring to life as part of your plan of redemption. You have so wonderfully blessed me in the wholesome simplicity of everyday living. I praise you for your delight in all of creation and thank you for swings and for other good and simple things. Amen.

$\mathcal{I}$ HATE YOU

Praise be to the God and Father of our Lord Jesus Christ, who has blessed us in the heavenly realms with every spiritual blessing in Christ.

—Ephesians 1:3

And I pray that you, being rooted and established in love, may have power, together with all the saints, to grasp how wide and long and high and deep is the love of Christ, and to know this love that surpasses knowledge—that you may be filled to the measure of all the fullness of God.

—Ephesians 3:17–19

I consider that our present sufferings are not worth comparing with the glory that will be revealed in us.

—Romans 8:18

IN THE REARVIEW MIRROR, I caught sight of Christiana as she held aloft the rubber figures of a bottle-nosed dolphin and a harbor dolphin. She lowered her voice into the lilting tones of a professional announcer. "Ladies and gentlemen, we welcome you to the Indianapolis Zoo's Whale and Dolphin Pavilion." She manipulated her performers in rapid leaps and plunges accompanied by the appropriate whooshing and splashing sounds.

We'd had a great day at the zoo. The sun was out and the animals were active—at least in the morning. We lucked into a close-up view of the elusive Bengal tigers and an impromptu show by the polar bear as he played with his giant red ball against the underwater viewing glass. All three children were happy and well behaved. We'd ridden on the elephant, the train, and the horse-drawn trolley. We'd eaten hotdogs and ice cream cones. And, as we left, I'd surprised them by buying them each something at the gift shop. Now the hues of the sunset in the rearview mirror held the promise of a beautiful ending to a perfect day.

Christiana continued the show. "Now, ladies and gentlemen, the dolphins will jump up and touch these balls with their noses." Aided by only Christiana's thumbs and forefingers the amazing rubber dolphins disappeared behind the back of the middle seat and then shot up, up, up until their noses touched the ceiling of the van. "Yaay! That was wonderful!"

Hannah, who shared the backseat with Christiana and the dolphins, had not applauded. Instead, she put her hands over her ears and screwed her face into a scowl. "Not so loud!"

Christiana continued the show, ignoring her sister's edict. The dolphins swam up and down and back and forth through their tank of airspace. "You know, ladies and gentlemen we must keep our water clean so the dolphins can live in the oceans."

"Mo-om," Hannah said, "Christiana won't stop."

"It's all right if she plays with her dolphins. Christiana, will you be a little quieter, please?"

Christiana looked into my eyes via the rearview mirror and nodded.

Hannah closed her animal dictionary and crossed her arms.

Christiana whooshed and splashed her dolphin pair in circles. As the dolphins neared the center of the van, I glanced once more into the mirror and caught sight of a fist that knocked one of the endangered species right out of the tank.

I witnessed the dastardly deed with weary disappointment. "Hannah!"

Hannah sank down in her seat. "Well, Christiana was putting her stupid dolphins on my side of the seat."

"Hannah, I was watching. Christiana did not put that dolphin anywhere near you. You will take a fifteen-minute time-out on the couch when you get home. You owe your sister an apology."

Hannah glared at Christiana. "Sor-ry."

"That didn't sound very sorry, Hannah."

"Well, I just can't do it then." Her eyes filled with tears. She wiped the back of her hand across her face and wailed, "You *always* get me in trouble instead of Christiana. It's not fair."

"Hannah, you know that's not true. We've had a long day, but you still need to be tolerant of other people. And hitting is never acceptable."

Hannah sniffed back her tears. "I hate you."

"Hannah, I don't think you mean that. We've had a wonderful day, and you're angry. But that's not a nice or respectful thing to say."

She looked out the window and whispered, "I do too hate you."

The last bit of color faded from the sky. Hannah would probably fuss and fume all evening and carry her stubborn pride to bed. I couldn't *make* her feel humble or repentant.

I doubted if Hannah knew what it was like to "hate," but I would have to wait until tomorrow to hear "I love you" again.

Reflections

We are so blessed! But when we take our blessings for granted and fail to have appreciation for all that God has given us, we get focused on life's irritations and unfair circumstances. We let them cancel our thanksgiving and steal away the joy of being loved and blessed by our heavenly Father. We lash out at others in self-pity, and we may even feel like God doesn't care about us at all.

Prayer

Dear God, sometimes I do have real problems, but most days my life is free of serious crises. Help me not to take for granted the rich blessings you provide for me every day. Thank you for the gift of a well body so that I was able to get out of bed today. Thank you for the security that I will not have to worry about hunger today. Thank you for the beauty of nature you have provided outside my window, for the song of the birds and the light of the sun. Thank you for the riches of your love in Christ Jesus. Help me to fill up my heart with your love and abundant provision so that I may weigh the effects of life's inconveniences lightly and face my problems with eternal perspective. Help me to experience the joy of living in your loving care. Amen.

PATHS IN THE SNOW

For this God is our God for ever and ever;
he will be our guide even to the end.

—Psalm 48:14

Therefore encourage one another and build each other
up. . . . Encourage the timid, help the weak, be patient
with everyone.

—1 Thessalonians 5:11, 14

Not that I have already obtained all this, or have al-
ready been made perfect, but I press on to take hold of
that for which Christ Jesus took hold of me. . . . Join with
others in following my example, . . . and take note of
those who live according to the pattern we gave you.

—Philippians 3:12, 17

I GAZED OUT THE WINDOW at the white landscape in our backyard. The blizzard had deposited so much snow that only the top rail
of the garden fence was visible. A crusty top layer of ice had been
sculpted by the wind into wavy drifts.

I needed a few minutes respite after twenty minutes of layering and
bundling giggly Hannah and wiggly Christiana. My elated explorers
had never seen snow this deep. I'd sent the girls out through the garage to the backyard close on the heels of Nathaniel who, as the eldest
sibling, proudly accepted the role of expedition leader.

Sophie, our beagle, was the first enthusiast to come into view. She skittered across the ice crust with the gusto of a puppy, poking her nose into the dusting of loose top snow, searching for the scent of a squirrel or rabbit. Then Nathaniel appeared. He labored down the short hill from the garage, breaking through the crust with each step. He was trying to match Sophie's run, but the snow pulled at his boots. He flailed his arms, trying to aid his momentum and balance himself.

"Brother!" Hannah called.

She and Christiana had stopped a few feet down from the top of the hill. With each step, they balanced on the layer of ice, then as they shifted their weight forward, their foot poked through the crust with a jolt. The uncertainty of when they were going to fall through had apparently unnerved them.

Nathaniel waved them forward. "Follow me. Step where I step."

The girls hesitated. Nathaniel threw up his arms and trudged back to where they stood. He took Hannah's hand and led her over to the path he had cut. Christiana and Hannah shuffled their way down the hill, holding onto each other for support. With Nathaniel in the lead they created a walkway through the trees to the back fence and then around the garden and back to the house. By the time they had circled the yard once they were swinging their arms and stomping their boots in grand parade style.

Within the next hour, the network of paths had grown to a major intra-yard system. The kids gathered broken chunks of ice from the crust and arranged them into a snow fort.

Hannah was now making her own paths, confidently stomping through the ice crust with great enthusiasm and gathering the ice chunks she created in the process of path-making.

She had just needed a little help getting started.

Reflections

When we are starting on a new venture with God we sometimes hesitate to call on him to break a path through the unnerving uncertainties before us. We think we should have the ability to do the task or exhibit a character trait, and we are impatient with ourselves when we don't live up to what we believe are God's expectations. But in any path down which he leads us, God never expects us to go without help. The whole New Testament is filled with exhortations to help and encourage one another. When we do ask for help, God often gently guides us with encouragement and support from a brother or sister in Christ.

Prayer

Dear God, thank you for leading me, for taking my hand and helping me to learn that the path on which you lead me is nothing to fear. Rather, it's an adventure into grace, hope, joy, and love. When you lead me in a new direction, some of the steps are unnerving, but help me to know that you are always there beside me when I call to you. Help me also to humble myself and look to your children who have gone before me, or to those who walk beside me, as an example, and for encouragement and support. Prepare me for the time when you may call me to be an example and support for others. Amen.

*J*ESUS IN MY WAY

Whether you turn to the right or to the left, your ears will hear a voice behind you, saying, "This is the way; walk in it."

—Isaiah 30:21

Those who [wait] in the LORD
will renew their strength.
They will soar on wings like eagles;
they will run and not grow weary,
they will walk and not be faint.

—Isaiah 40:31

THE RED MERCURY WAS clearly visible against the white back-drop of the freshly fallen snow. The thermometer that hung outside the window read twenty-eight degrees—not too cold for a winter day in Indiana.

"All right kids, time to get your coats on," I called back to the kids in the bathroom. The children mumbled their acknowledgments through mouths full of foamy toothpaste. "Time to go out and wait for the bus."

Christiana rinsed her toothbrush and tossed it into her drawer. "It's too cold!"

The closet door squeaked open. I began the search for coats and mittens. "You'll be all right. Nathaniel has shoveled a path. Look, the bus will be here any minute."

I pulled out three heavy hooded coats and did a quick pocket check.

"Good. Mittens are in your pockets. Please return them to your pockets when you get to school."

Nathaniel and Hannah grasped the cuffs of their sweaters as they pulled on their winter coats, then sorted out which mitten belonged to which hand.

Christiana crossed her arms.

I held out Christiana's coat. "Come on, Christiana. Grab your sleeves."

"It's too cold." She jumped up and down.

"Right now, or there'll be consequences."

Christiana snorted like a confounded bull. She uncrossed her arms and jerked on her coat. Fishing up her sleeves to pull down her crumpled sweatshirt, I wondered at the same time why I was doing this for her; she wasn't even complaining about scrunched up sleeves.

"Go out the side door so you don't have as far to walk."

The troops stomped through the kitchen and out the door, Christiana trailing.

I stood inside the storm door watching the winter expedition proceed toward the street. "Be careful not to fall—and stay out of the unshoveled part of the driveway. You don't have your snow boots on."

I closed the storm door and wrapped my robe tighter around me. I was looking forward to a quiet morning at home and a hot shower. Don had already left for work in our only vehicle.

I walked to the bedroom to gather my clothes, and out the window I saw the children waiting for the bus. Nathaniel had shoveled a path down the driveway, and had cleared a six-by-nine-foot waiting area. Hannah stood facing the street, searching for the bus, ready to board. Nathaniel swung his lunch box from side to side, testing the distance between himself and his sisters, edging for a few tense moments into contact range.

Christiana, her arms crossed, danced around the rectangle. Nathaniel said something to her that sparked an angry response. She stomped toward the path, but Nathaniel stepped ahead of Christiana, blocking her retreat. Christiana lowered her eyebrows and shook her head, leaving little doubt that her remarks to Nathaniel were beyond a polite complaint. Nathaniel, however, held his ground. Christiana jumped up and down in quick spurts. Then she walked up to Nathaniel and stepped to the side, staring around him and contemplating the foot-deep snow toward the house.

Oh, please don't miss the bus this morning. I'm not dressed. I don't have the van.

Nathaniel pointed to the snow, and evidently gave Christiana some more unwelcome brotherly advice. She stuck out her tongue and turned her back on him, but she didn't venture out into the snow to get around his roadblock. I was sure her rude tongue had not gone unnoticed by Nathaniel and prayed that he would not respond by resuming his lunch-box swinging—with a target in mind.

The bus rounded the corner, calling for a truce. All attention was focused on the promise of heated transport. Christiana jumped up and down a couple more times, but took her place in the boarding line behind Hannah. Nathaniel stepped from his roadblock position to third in line.

Sibling conflict brought on by a bossy brother was not my favorite situation to deal with, but for once I was thankful my hot-blooded daughter had a big brother to stand in her way.

Reflections

We all reach the place on our journey with God when we feel like we're just waiting—not doing much growing or performing fruitful ministry. But God's timing is perfect for every action and season of growth. God sends opportunities for ministry or spiritual development when we're ready and when the situation is just right. When we try to thwart God's plan by retreating back into the past or lunging ahead, God may block our way to keep us from missing his leading. At such times it's easy, in our fast-paced society, to get frustrated with God.

Even in short waiting times, we can respond with impatience and anxiety, or we can respond with restful anticipation. Learning to wait with grace in our daily lives can help us carry the same attitude into times of spiritual transition.

Prayer

Dear God, sometimes I'm like an impatient child waiting for the bus. I get restless and cold waiting for you to pick me up and take me to the next destination on the journey with you. I jump up and down and complain that I want to go back to the warm familiar places. At those times, you often block my retreat, and I realize that there's no going back unless I want to get off of the path you have made for me and go it alone. Help me to wait patiently for you to come, knowing that you always do come when the time is right, to lead me on our journey together. Thank you for your faithful guidance. Amen.

A CHILD OF ALL AGES

There is a time for everything,
and a season for every activity under heaven.

—Ecclesiastes 3:1

"DO I HAVE TO GO TO CHOIR?"

"Yes, Nathaniel," I said. "You have to go to choir."

He pounded his dinner roll against his plate, and I stared at his bread-flattening ritual in amusement. "Um, Passover isn't for another couple of months."

"Humph?" He stuffed a bite of bread in his mouth and shook his head.

"You know . . . Passover . . . unleavened bread."

He tilted his head and scowled at me.

"Unleavened bread is flat like your smashed roll." Still the blank stare. "I was making a little joke."

"A *very* little joke."

"Nathaniel, don't be disrespectful," Don said.

"Why do I have to go to choir? I'm twelve. I can stay home by myself."

"It's only one hour a week, Nathaniel," said Don. "It's part of serving at the church. It's good to do some things just because it's right even if it's not your favorite thing to do."

"I hate it!"

"Come on." I tried to sound cheerful. "It's not that bad." I thought, *My poor tone-deaf son. I wish this wasn't so hard on him, but Don is right.*

"It's not fair." Nathaniel finished off his roll and stared at his plate.

"I like choir," Hannah said.

"Me too," Christiana nodded.

"We know *you* like to sing." Nathaniel glared.

"Everyone has different strengths," I said. "Now, let's clear the table. We don't want to be late." I carried the bowls of mashed potatoes and green beans into the kitchen.

Don picked up the roll basket. "Come on, Nathaniel. You need to get the leftovers put away."

Nathaniel shoved his chair as he left the table.

"I'll help you." I spooned the green beans into a plastic storage bowl.

Nathaniel picked up a bowl in slow motion and plopped two-thirds of the potatoes into the dish. The rest went on the counter. I decided not to comment. Then I noticed his bare feet.

"Nathaniel, you haven't even gotten your shoes on. We need to leave in just a few minutes."

"I'm not going!"

I stepped back to get a better look at my son. Could this rebellious child be my gentle, obedient boy? He snapped the lid on the potatoes without looking up.

"I thought your father and I made it clear that we expect you to go to choir tonight. Get your shoes on. I'll finish putting away the food."

Nathaniel huffed and flung the serving spoon in the sink on his way out of the kitchen. But he did retrieve his shoes from the foyer and sit down to put them on. *Well, here it is, the teenage years.* That scene could have been out of a textbook on teenage attitudes.

I remembered when Nathaniel was two and was asserting his will. We had to use safety pins on his pajamas so he wouldn't unzip them and take them off at bedtime. And we had to restrain his little hands, as he was determined to unlatch his car seat. I'd almost forgotten what a strong will he had when he was going through that stage. I told Don then how thankful I was that the two-year-old stage didn't last forever. And it didn't. It gave way to the four-year-old "Why's" and then to the paper-cutting, Play-Doh smashing, game-playing energetic young boy. Now Nathaniel was a preteen, and the see-saw between assertion and seeking affirmation, searching out his self-identity had begun.

"Duh, duh, dah dah . . . ," Nathaniel sang as he trotted out of the church after choir. He was smiling and swinging his coat around in time to the tune.

"So, how was choir?" I asked.

He shrugged. "It was all right."

"Not too bad?" Don said.

"It was OK. Hey, Hannah, race you to the van." He darted away.

Hannah ran after him. "It doesn't count. You got a head start!"

"Yes, it does," he yelled back.

"I guess choir wasn't so bad after all," I said.

Reflections

We speak about our conversion experiences as our time of new birth in Christ—complete in the sense of the finished work of Jesus on the cross, yet a beginning for us in our new lives and relationships as God's children. Spiritual life isn't lineal; physical years aren't necessarily a measure of spiritual maturity. Some Christians never get beyond the struggle to just have trust in God, while other Christians seem to find faith easy but struggle more with obedience, letting go, or other issues related to their deepening faith.

When my children are exhibiting undesirable behaviors that are normal in a stage of development, I'm often comforted by the knowledge that this is just a stage they are going through and not a permanent part of their personality. God doesn't expect us to spiritually grow up in an instant.

Prayer

Dear God, just like my children, sometimes my behaviors and attitudes are like a two-year-old—I strain to assert my will over yours and pout when I don't get my way. Sometimes I'm like a four-year-old, doubting every precept of your Word and spending all of my energies questioning you, asking you "Why?" Sometimes I'm a happy, creative energetic child, enjoying life and new growth and accomplishments. Sometimes I'm like a teenager, rebelling at your authority and at the same time longing for your approval, struggling to find my identity as your child. Thank you for loving me through all of my stages of spiritual growth and for seeing the real "me," whom you have created, beyond all of my growing and changing. Amen.

HONESTLY . . .

Search me, O God, and know my heart;
test me and know my anxious thoughts.
See if there is any offensive way in me,
and lead me in the way everlasting.

—Psalm 139:23–24

Speaking the truth in love, we will in all things grow up
into him who is the Head, that is, Christ.

—Ephesians 4:15

Love must be sincere.

—Romans 12:9

CHRISTIANA CALLED TO the front of the van, "How long until we get there?"

Our family had driven ten-and-a-half hours since leaving Indiana to visit my sister and her family in Virginia.

I reached over and rubbed the back of Don's neck. "Ten minutes less than the last time you asked."

Nathaniel looked up from his reading and closed his book. "That would make it only five minutes 'til we get there."

I leaned around the seat to see the faces of my three road-weary children. "Good job on the math. Now it's time for the standard going-to-relatives lecture from Mom."

Hannah put up her hand, signaling me to stop. "Don't tell me. Don't tell me. Say please and thank you, especially for the food, even if you don't like it."

I laughed. My sister and her family were healthy eaters. She ground her own wheat to make homemade bread; they ate very little meat and drank water at meals.

"Pretty much, but you don't need to tell Aunt Tonya you liked something if you didn't. Please just try—"

"—a little of everything."

"Yes, Hannah. Please don't interrupt. *And,* if you can't honestly say thank you for the food, say thank you for preparing the meal. You can always appreciate the work people do for you because they care about you—even if the results aren't your favorite.

"You know, I had a friend who used to come over to my house when I was a child. She was very polite, but sometimes she was so polite she wasn't honest."

"But lying isn't polite," Hannah said.

"No. That's true. I don't think she meant to lie exactly. She was just doing what she'd been taught. She called my mom, 'Mrs. Helms' and she said 'Yes, ma'am,' and 'Thank you,' but I don't think she really was very thankful."

I thought back to the scene, which was much the same every time my friend came over:

"Thank you for the lunch, Mrs. Helms," Angela said. "I really enjoyed it."

My mother glanced at Angela's plate. The macaroni and cheese had merely been picked apart, and the apple slices barely nibbled on.

"Thank you," my mom said. "Are you sure you've eaten enough?"

"Oh yes, ma'am. I'm full." She nodded her head and pushed her chair back from the table.

"But you've only eaten a couple of bites. Maybe you could finish your milk?"

Angela picked up the half-full cup and obediently drank the remainder. "May I please be excused?"

"Me, too, Mom?" I asked (my plate being empty).

"All right, girls. If you're sure you've had enough. Take your plates into the kitchen."

"Don't you like macaroni and cheese?" I asked as we delivered our plates to the kitchen counter.

"Sure, but my mom makes the kind out of the box," said Angela, "and she always peels my apples."

Pulling into my sister's long driveway, I pondered my friend's behavior once again. She had been taught to be polite at the cost of her honesty, but she likely didn't think of it that way. She probably just said the words "Thank you," "I enjoyed it," and "I'm full" without thinking much at all. Perhaps she had learned that saying the right words got her out of eating and on to playing. Or perhaps she was afraid that my mom would yell at her, or that I wouldn't like her if she didn't say those things. I would never know.

I hoped I could teach my children to be honest—and polite.

Reflections

How honest are we with God? In church we repeat phrases like "Thank you, Jesus," "Praise you, God," "We worship you, Lord." But do we sometimes forget the meaning behind the words? We're rewarded with the acceptance and esteem of others when we use these phrases often, when we can share stories that beam with spiritual victories, or when others see us as kind and loving people. Such responses can lead us to believe that to be acceptable children in God's family, only positive feelings, words, and experiences are allowed at church and in our relationship with God. If we're not careful, then, we will become dishonest about the normal negative experiences in our lives, the less than loving thoughts and feelings, and the tears and fears and struggles that we all go through.

In reality, our relationship with God calls for us above all else to be honest with God and with ourselves. God's love is able to encompass all of the experiences, thoughts, and feelings in our lives, both positive and negative. The writers of the Psalms expressed with exuberation both their praises of God and their honest fears, laments, and even anger.

The writers of the epistles instruct Christians to be present with each other both in rejoicing and weeping (Rom. 12:15). We are also instructed to be angry but not to sin (Eph. 4:26). Should we be polite and discerning about our sharing in the church? Of course. And honest? Yes, but always "speaking the truth in love."

Prayer

Dear God, help me to be a truthful child. Help me to trust your love and understanding. Help me not to try to impress you with my goodness or strength, but to have the courage to be honest with you and with myself about my desires and feelings. In times when my feelings and desires don't align with your loving will, give me the courage to confess my faults to you. You already know my deepest heart. Transform me into your pleasing child, living within the freedom of truth, without deceit. Amen.

$\mathcal{P}$ATIENT SNOWFLAKES

Be imitators of God, therefore, as dearly loved children and live a life of love, just as Christ loved us and gave himself up for us as a fragrant offering and sacrifice to God.

—Ephesians 5:1–2

I tell you the truth, anyone who has faith in me will do what I have been doing. He will do even greater things than these, because I am going to the Father.

—John 14:12

THE FRONT DOOR jerked open with a rasp, pulling my attention from the picture of the lion on the *National Geographic* renewal notice. Sorting the mail was my daily ritual while I waited for the school bus to bring my children home. I used the time to transition from the quiet household of semi-organized work to the response-driven mode of motherhood.

"Hi, Mom." Hannah was first through the door today—unusual. "Can I have some coffee filters? We—"

"Mommy!" Christiana bounded into the room, dropped her school bag, and crushed the paper lion against my chest in her enthusiastic embrace.

"Just a minute, Christiana. Let me put this down."

Hannah put her hands on her hips. "Christiana, I was talking to Mom."

Christiana pulled away and smiled at me, apparently not hearing or caring about her sister's indignation.

I returned her "I love you" in my smile but reprimanded, "Christiana, your sister's right; you did interrupt."

Christiana turned and noticed Hannah for the first time. "Sorry."

Usually, Christiana ran in before Hannah, gave me my daily hug, and then headed outside for her afternoon swinging session.

She released me and headed for the back door.

I picked up Christiana's purple canvas, Winnie-the-Pooh school bag. "Please take this to your room first."

Christiana grabbed Winnie and bolted.

"Now, Hannah, you were asking for coffee filters? Aren't you a little young for coffee?"

"Mo-om. At school today we made snowflakes from them."

"Oh. Well, you're in luck. I just bought a huge package of filters from the wholesale store, so I have extras you may have." I stood on my tiptoes to reach my stash of paper goods.

Hannah plopped her school bag down on the bench and fished around for her scissors.

I handed her a stack of the flimsy paper circles. "That's a great idea. We always had to cut the corners out when we made paper snow-flakes."

"You made snowflakes when you were in school?"

"Of course, Hannah. They did have snow even way back then, even in Alabama on occasion."

Hannah gave me a courtesy grin and shook her head. She worked one of the filters loose and sat down at the kitchen table to focus on her task. I pulled a pair of household scissors out of the catch-all drawer and sat across from her.

"I used to love to make snowflakes." I fiddled loose a filter and fol-lowed Hannah in folding it into a pie shape. I paused for a moment, remembering the process. First an inward acute angle cut off the point—that would make a pretty star shape in the center. Then . . . let's see . . . two point to point half hearts on one side and a matching pair staggered on the opposite side, leaving uniform spaces of filter paper between. Close to the outer edge, a triangle on each side with slightly swirled intertwining tips—sort of a yin/yang look. The outer edge I'll echo the curve of the heart center with points between coming up on either side.

"This is great! The filter paper is—"

I looked up to see Hannah staring at me, mouth slightly open. She had folded her filter but had apparently been observing my invention instead of creating her own work of winter artistry.

"—um, so easy to cut. Hannah, why aren't you making one too?"

"I want to see yours."

"All right." I started unfolding the translucent star. "Hannah, you're just in the second grade. I've been doing this for a long time."

I finished unfolding and smoothed my snowflake out on the table.

Hannah pulled it over in front of her. "I like it. I want one just like yours."

"You just have fun making your own snowflakes. You know, they say no two snowflakes are exactly alike."

"Mo-om."

"OK. Well, I've got things to do. Have fun."

I passed Hannah several times during the afternoon.

"Mom, how did you do that?" I stopped and refolded my flake to show her the heart cut.

"Mom, look! Mine doesn't look anything like yours!" I showed her how she did the correct cut, but backward, assuring her she would get it right on the next one.

"Mom, my snowflake fell apart. I hate this!" I showed her how she hadn't left any uncut space between her hearts and encouraged her to try again.

"Hannah, have patience with yourself. I've been at snowflake making a long time. You'll get it, just maybe not today."

"But I want to make one like yours!" Hannah pursed her lips and picked up her scissors.

"OK." I went into the living room to fold laundry. I heard several heavy sighs and a couple of thumps on the table, but no calls for help.

Twenty minutes later Hannah appeared in the doorway, holding aloft a snowflake. It sported a pattern of mirrored hearts and diamonds with opposing swirled tips.

I pushed the pile of unmatched socks from my lap. "You've done it!"

Hannah handed me the snowflake; her freckled cheeks bunched up in a pleased grin.

I noticed the hearts were different sizes so that the spaces between weren't quite even, and the diamonds had a little notch where the scissors hadn't gotten turned all the way around. The star in the center was a bit larger than mine had been. But it was a beautiful snowflake, made most definitely after the pattern of my own.

I pulled Hannah to me in a side hug. "Well, that's just beautiful."

"Just like yours?"

"Just like mine."

Reflections

When we read Scripture and imagine all of the wonderful works God wants to bring about through our lives, we sometimes feel unsatisfied with the works we see in our lives now. Through God's living in Jesus Christ as an example before us, we can see his perfect love and compassion, his wondrous wisdom and discernment, his beauty as creator and redeemer. Our attempts at imitating God seem meager, shabby, and defective in comparison. Reflecting God's nature comes from a lifetime of practicing his presence, abiding in him. We need to be patient with ourselves as we grow up in our relationship with God as his "dearly loved children."

Prayer

Dear God, it's natural for me as your child to want to imitate your works. Help me to listen carefully to your instruction from your Word and through the Holy Spirit. Help me to realize that you value my imitation of you, and encourage me to follow your example as you continually create my unique self. Help me to know that your first priority in relationship is in loving who I am, not in judging what I can do. Thank you for your patient teaching and encouragement. Amen.

*W*IDOW'S MITES AND M&MS

As he looked up, Jesus saw the rich putting their gifts into the temple treasury. He also saw a poor widow put in two very small copper coins. "I tell you the truth," he said, "this poor widow has put in more than all the others. All these people gave their gifts out of their wealth; but she out of her poverty put in all she had to live on."
—Luke 21:1–4

I am God, your God. . . .
The world is mine, and all that is in it. . . .
He who sacrifices thank offerings honors me,
and he prepares the way
so that I may show him the salvation of God.
—Psalm 50:7, 12, 23

"HANNAH," I CALLED FROM the bathroom, "you forgot to clean the back of the toilet. Please come and finish your work."

Hannah continued playing the piano.

"Hannah, I mean right now."

"OK, in just a minute."

Hannah's "minutes" often stretched into hours—or days—of forgetfulness.

"No. Now, Hannah."

The piano sounded a discord. "Oh, all right."

"Watch your attitude. No one is mistreating you here. Housework is part of living in the house."

I handed Hannah her cleaning cloth and spray as she shuffled into the bathroom. Then I opened the closet to inspect Christiana's job of emptying the trash can. The can was empty, but a collection of tissues and cotton swabs littered the floor. I found Christiana sweeping the stairs to the basement.

"Christiana, when you finish here I need you to go back to the bathroom and pick up around the trash can."

Christiana slammed the whisk broom down on a step. "Work, work, work! I already did that!"

"You know that you need to clean up around the trash cans. If you'd done the job right in the first place, you wouldn't have to redo it—and if you slam or throw anything more, you'll be taking a time-out on the couch."

Christiana pursed her lips and clenched her fists but controlled any further outburst of temper.

"None of you are being mistreated here. Your work really doesn't take that long, and then you can play the rest of the day."

"No. I've got to clean my room."

"That's true. It does need to be in condition to be vacuumed. But I've seen you clean it pretty quickly when you get with it."

I made my way back up the stairs and looked over the furniture in the living room. Nathaniel had done a fairly good job dusting, but the magazines and books that had been stacked on the tables were lying on the floor. I started to pick them up myself and then succumbed to the nagging voice in my mind: *If you do it for them they'll never learn to do it themselves.* I argued back, *But, it's easier to do it myself.* Nevertheless, I dropped the *National Geographic* and went to find Nathaniel.

After an hour-and-a-half of watching my children do housework, I felt exhausted. But the house was clean and the clutter, well, it was at least redistributed into less visible locations. I rejoiced at being able to relax my slave driver's whip for another week.

"Hannah, Christiana, Nathaniel, come here."

"What?" Hannah called from her room. Christiana peeked her head around the corner and looked down the hall to where I was standing in the kitchen.

"Y'all come here. I have something for you."

Nathaniel hopped off of the couch and walked in, still reading his book. The gathering of the troops was complete.

I pulled out a bag of M&M candies. "It's just a little something to thank you for your good work."

"All right!" Nathaniel put his book on the counter and put out his hand.

Hannah's eyes brightened as her hand came alongside her brother's.

"How many can I have?" asked Christiana.

I carefully poured the treasured candies onto a plate.

"*May* I have. We'll have to count."

Negotiations ensued for possession of the two rare blue M&Ms, then the happy candy misers disappeared from the kitchen.

"What do you say?" I called after them.

A chorus of chocolate-muted "Thank yous" followed.

I slouched onto the kitchen bench, trying to figure out which of the dozen jobs on my to-do list was the priority.

Christiana reappeared and leaned in silence against the doorjamb next to my shoulder.

"Mommy?"

"Yes, honey." I answered, but my eyes and my mind stayed on my list.

"These are for you." One orange and one yellow M&M rolled onto my list.

Splotches of brown showed through where the candy coating had melted onto Christiana's hand. Their culinary appeal had decreased considerably, but their value had increased immeasurably with their release into my keeping.

I pulled my daughter close and returned her bright smile.

"Thank you for sharing, Christiana."

Reflections

As God's children, what kind of gift can we give to our awesome heavenly parent to say "Thank you" for loving us and caring for us, just for being God, our God?

If we never experienced unconditional love and approval in our earthly childhood, we may find it difficult to believe that God values us or anything we give. True, our little gifts of love are not needed by God any more than we need a couple of half-melted M&Ms. But knowing how sweet our children's gifts are to us can help us realize God's delight in all that we give to him from our hearts. Just as with Christiana's candy offering, our gifts to God represent fountains of precious love from our hearts, love that our Father cherishes. Knowing that God treasures our gifts, most often given in his name to others, will encourage us to be more giving and loving persons.

Prayer

Dear God, my perspective is often cluttered with the pressures and expectations that define my worth in the eyes of this world. Thank you for always seeing the intent of my heart and evaluating my meager gifts in light of your love and truth. Help me to hold as a treasure every half-melted M&M, every hug, and every love note scribbled in crayon from my children. Doing so lets them know they are valued by me, and reminds me of how much you delight in my giving to you. From my heart full of love and thanksgiving, my dear heavenly parent, I offer this gift of praise to you today. Amen.

$\mathcal{A}$N ONLY CHILD

Praise be to the God and Father of our Lord Jesus Christ,
who has blessed us in the heavenly realms with every
spiritual blessing in Christ. For he chose us in him be-
fore the creation of the world to be holy and blameless
in his sight. In love he predestined us to be adopted as
his sons [and daughters] through Jesus Christ, in ac-
cordance with his pleasure and will—to the praise of
his glorious grace, which he has freely given us in the
One he loves.

—Ephesians 1:3–6

What do you think? If a man owns a hundred sheep,
and one of them wanders away, will he not leave the
ninety-nine on the hills and go to look for the one that
wandered off? And if he finds it, I tell you the truth, he
is happier about that one sheep than about the ninety-
nine that did not wander off. In the same way your Fa-
ther in heaven is not willing that any of these little ones
should be lost.

—Matthew 18:12–14

THE DOOR TO THE dining hall banged shut behind me. Stand-ing on the porch, I looked from the basketball court to the cabins, trying to decided where to go. I opted to step to the side and sit on one of the benches that lined the long dining hall porch. In a moment, two girls from my cabin, followed closely by Christiana, stepped out through the swinging doors. They started for the basketball courts, but Christiana stopped and looked around.

I waved. "Over here, Christiana."

She smiled and stepped toward me.

"Why don't you go over to the basketball courts with Cayla and Amanda?"

"Are you coming?"

"Not right now," I said. I'd been serving as cabin counselor at Camp Challenge, and was glad for a respite. "I just want to sit here for a couple of minutes."

Christiana scrutinized me for a moment. "Are you angry?"

"No. What makes you think I'm angry?"

"Are you upset?"

"No, honey. I'm fine. I've just been with you kiddos all day long and I wanted to sit by myself for a minute. Look," I smiled assurances and nodded toward the courts, "they're playing Knock Out. You're pretty good at that. Why don't you go on over? I'll be there in just a few minutes."

Christiana sat down next to me. "I want to be with Mommy."

"All right. But let's just be quiet for a little while. Mommy needs a break."

Christiana leaned on my shoulder and I put my arm around her. She's like a barometer, able in a remarkable way to gauge the rising and falling of my emotions. She always seemed to know when something was bothering me. We were in our second day of the week-long camp, enjoying the swimming, hiking, and the daily visit to the snack bar. On the other hand, amidst the fun, Christiana's difficulty in fitting in with the other children, her hurt feelings, and a screaming bout after being stung by a sweat bee had frayed my nerves. Bothering me most, however, was something to do with home.

"Christiana, do you remember that it's your brother's birthday today?"

"Oh, yeah."

"It's sort of a bummer not being able to be there, you know. I think this is the first time I've missed any of your birthdays."

"But we had cake before we left."

"I know. Still it's not the same as being there on the day. But this was the only week we could make it to camp, so . . ."

We sat in silence for a few seconds. I'd always loved going to church camp; I enjoyed being out in the woods, and not cooking for the week. But being a cabin counselor was a bit more taxing than I'd anticipated. Overall, though, I was glad we'd come.

I thought out loud, "Well, I suppose you can't be in two places at the same time."

Silence again.

Christiana sat up and looked at me. "Do you think brother's angry at you?"

It was sweet for her to be concerned. "No. I'm sure he understands, but he did seem a little disappointed when I told him we'd be gone."

Christiana's eyes brightened and she pointed at the snack bar. "Let's buy Nathaniel something."

I raised my eyebrows. "You're very generous with my money."

Christiana laughed.

"Good idea. Right now, though, let's head to the courts and join the others. Maybe today will be your lucky day at Knock Out."

Christiana pecked my cheek. "Thanks for coming to camp with me, Mommy."

I gave her a quick squeeze. "Well, thank you for thanking me."

"Thank you for thanking me for thanking—"

I stood and pulled her to her feet. "OK. OK. OK."

Reflections

Time. Time. Time! We never seem to have enough of it, and we have to choose what we do and what we don't do. If we have more than one child, limited time and energy sometimes means choosing between our children and their activities. In spite of how much we love each of our children, we're limited parents in a limited world. I suppose that's one advantage of having only one child or being an only child.

The good news about being a child of God is that God is outside time and is unlimited in love and energy. And God, through Jesus, has made a way for us to always be with him. Jesus said that even if ninety-nine are safe, he will come and search for the one lost soul. Every individual is so precious and important to God that he would give himself to save just that person. Even though God has billions of children to love, each of us is like an only child to our heavenly parent.

Prayer

Dear God, how wonderful and almost unbelievable that you, the maker of the universe, the creator of billions of individuals, loves me and looks upon me as if I am an only child, precious in your sight! Help me to snuggle in and enjoy your love, to fill up with your love—and praise you, praise you, praise you! Amen.

DEFINING GOD

Now faith is being sure of what we hope for and certain of what we do not see.

—Hebrews 11:1

The Almighty is beyond our reach and exalted in power.

—Job 37:23

DON CLIMBED THE stairs from his basement office and strode into the kitchen. Dirty dishes cluttered the counter, piles of papers littered the table—Tamara was gone on retreat with her seminary Women's Spirituality class.

"OK, kids, into the car," he announced. "We're going to Taco Bell for supper."

"All right!" Nathaniel answered from the living room.

Don headed down the hall toward the bedrooms. "Christiana, Hannah, let's go."

"Just a minute." Hannah's distracted tone said, "I'm reading this book at an exciting part."

Don stepped into the room. "Bring your book. You can read in the van."

In the van on the way to the restaurant, Christiana and Nathaniel thought aloud from the backseat, debating what they would order and relaying the information to Don. Hannah was silent, her book before her eyes.

"Hannah," Don said, "What do you want at Taco Bell?"

"What? Oh." Hannah's gaze stayed glued to her book. "I guess two soft tacos, no lettuce."

"Quite the book you're reading there."

Hannah put down her book. "I finished."

"What is it?"

"It's a Cam Jansen book, a mystery thing about dinosaur bones at a museum."

"A detective story?"

"Yeah, sort of. I like trying to figure out the problem before she does."

"I like mysteries too."

The van was quiet for a couple of seconds.

"Why doesn't the Bible say anything about dinosaurs?" Hannah asked.

"Where did that come from?"

"I was just thinking about things we don't know. I ask Mommy about God, but she doesn't seem to know the answers."

Don repressed a laugh. "Really? You mean she actually says she doesn't know anything?"

"Well, not exactly. But, when I ask her something like 'How does God talk to us?' she says maybe this, and sometimes that, and she doesn't just tell me."

"Well, God isn't a person like us, and so God is sometimes difficult to understand."

The van pulled into the Taco Bell parking lot.

Hannah unsnapped her seat belt. "But I want to know."

"I guess knowing about God is sort of like your mystery book— you know some things while you're reading the story, but you have to wait until the end to get the full answer."

Nathaniel slid open the side door "'The end'—that means with God, like when you're dead."

Hannah rolled her eyes. "Oh brother. You guys sound just like Mom."

Reflections

We sometimes find ourselves trying to squeeze God into a definition we can understand. We probably don't do this consciously, but whenever we catch ourselves feeling complacent about God we need to reexamine our image of God. God is mystery.

Yes, our gracious and loving God has given us a reflection of himself in creation, and he sent Jesus to let us know, on a relational level, what God is like. Still, we must always remember we are the created of God, limited in understanding of the Source of all our being. We must be on guard against letting ourselves slip from being precious children created in God's image to deceived children, looking for the comfortable control we feel when we create God in our image.

Prayer

Dear God, you are my Creator, the Creator of everything in this universe. I catch a glimpse of how awesome you are through the variety and detail, the colors and textures of your creation. I stand in awe and then fall to my knees before you when I think about how you have revealed yourself through Jesus; your perfect nature of love is, indeed, defined in Jesus. Yet you are still so beyond my understanding. The paradox in your nature makes my head spin. Sometimes I'm very uncomfortable in not being able to figure you out, to put you into a neat package with all the loose ends tied up. Help me to let go of needing to know those things you have chosen to keep unknown. Help me to trust your love when doubts—arising from misunderstanding—threaten to rob me of faith. You are so wonderful. I worship you today as my God. In Jesus' name. Amen.

THE RACE: I JUST WANT HER TO DO WELL (PART 1)

In all my prayers for all of you, I always pray with joy because of your partnership in the gospel from the first day until now, being confident of this, that he who began a good work in you will carry it on to completion until the day of Christ Jesus.

—Philippians 1:4–6

"For I know the plans I have for you," declares the LORD, "plans to prosper you and not to harm you, plans to give you hope and a future."

—Jeremiah 29:11

I SWIPED AT A CRUMB on the kitchen counter. It missed my hand and bounced onto the floor. Tossing the sponge into the sink, I returned to the task of clearing the counter. The school papers, event notices, and bills to be sorted sprawled out next to the toast crumbs, daring me to delve into their deferred demands. I turned my back on them and leaned against the counter. Staring out the kitchen window was all I had energy for. And as I gazed at the fields, now a young green of spring, I thought about my dear Christiana, our very different daughter, who wanted so desperately to fit in with others, to have something she did well.

Christiana's younger sister, Hannah, was gifted academically. We were discovering that she also had unusual musical ability. She had just begun taking piano lessons and was jumping ahead by leaps and bounds. It was easy to "ooh" and "aah" over Hannah's musical abilities and her straight "A" report cards.

Christiana's older brother, Nathaniel, was also academically gifted and had been the Indiana sixth-grade Scholastic Chess Champion the previous year. He had been winning at scholastic chess since he was in second grade and had a room full of ribbons and trophies—big, fancy trophies and shiny ribbons that thrilled Christiana.

"Why can't I have a trophy? It's not fair!"

I was so tired of hearing that lament from her; and so tired of trying to explain why she had been born with the limitations of a mild mental handicap, with the added complications of an autistic spectrum disorder. I really believed mental ability wasn't the most important and that loving others, which she could do well, was much more crucial to having a full and happy life. But convincing her that her value lay in being exactly who God made her to be was very difficult. Her autism made her a tactile learner. Even more than most children, external rewards were important to her; my words meant very little without a trophy to back them up.

Today, Christiana would have a chance to do well at something in the physical realm. Today, Christiana could win a ribbon. Today was the annual Anderson Elementary School Field Day, where all the elementary schools competed in a one-day track and field event. Christiana had been practicing after school with her team and had been running the 400 meter race in very good time. She had the long legs of a runner, and in this event her autism, which made her tend to be oblivious to pain when she was focused on a goal, was in her favor. Her coaches were careful not to push her too hard but, more than some of the other students, she was apt to push herself past her comfort zone.

The big hurdle for her now was the starting gun. The sudden pop terrified her. One aspect of autism is sensory integration dysfunction, which meant, in this case, that what might sound to us like a little pop sounded to her like a howitzer. She had integrated so much over the past few years and could tolerate many more ear-grating noises than she used to. I hoped she could handle it this year. I knew that the trophies and the ribbons and the praises of people are not of lasting importance, yet it would be so great for her to feel that she could do something well. I sniffed back the tears, feeling the pain of watching her struggle with her feelings of self-worth. She was such a precious child.

But what if she just couldn't do it today—another failure, another disappointment.

"I ache for her, Lord. I just want her to do well. I don't know if you understand . . ." I stopped my prayer as I heard myself talking to my heavenly Father, whom I imagined stood with raised eyebrows, bemused at the absurdity of my doubt. The peace of heavenly abundance washed over me.

"Of course you understand. She was your child before she was mine. You love her and have a plan for her far beyond this day's event. Thank you for caring for my precious Christiana."

Reflections

God wants us, his children, to do well. Could it be that God aches for each of us as we struggle to live the Christian life, as we face failures and seek to find and fulfill our gifts? Although living the Christian life is about worshipping and serving God, Jesus said that the result of God-focused living is an abundant life. Yes, we will sometimes be called upon to suffer for Christ's sake, but even in those times we can experience the abundance of God's peace and grace. We don't need to feel guilty when we're successful and joyful. God is rooting for us and is ready to enable us to do well in all things for his glory, that together our joy may be full.

Prayer

Dear God, you want me to do well, to succeed using the gifts and abilities you have given to me. I sometimes let the old adage, "If you're grinning, you're sinning," hold me back from excelling in my life. Sometimes I get mixed up, thinking that I won't be humble if I'm too successful, even in the work you have given me to do. Help me to hold in sacred stewardship the abundant life Jesus bought for me at such a high cost, and to rejoice with you in my successes. In Jesus' name, Amen.

*T*HE RACE: COURAGE IN THE RACE (PART 2)

Therefore, since we are surrounded by such a great cloud of witnesses, let us throw off everything that hinders and the sin that so easily entangles, and let us run with perseverance the race marked out for us. Let us fix our eyes on Jesus, the author and perfecter of our faith.

—Hebrews 12:1–2

Love the LORD, *all his saints!*
The LORD *preserves the faithful. . . .*
Be strong and take heart,
all you who hope in the LORD.

—Psalm 31:23–24

I GRIPPED THE STEERING wheel with both hands and leaned forward. Taking a deep breath, I tried to relax. Having just picked up Hannah from school, we were on our way to the local high school track for the annual elementary field day competition. Christiana was scheduled to run the 400-meter race. The event was meant to be fun, a no-big-deal way of introducing the upper grade elementary students to track and field. I shouldn't be so tense, but with Christiana nothing was "no big deal"—everything was a major event.

"Do I have to come?" Hannah asked.

"Yes. And Papa's going to meet us there. Your sister has worked really hard at practices to be able to run this race and we need to support her. You know Christiana has wanted to run track for the past two years, and she's a good runner, but she's afraid of the noise of the starting gun."

"It's just a little pop gun."

"For us it's just a little pop gun, but for her it sounds more like a cannon or the scraping of fingernails on a chalkboard, you know, a noise that really gets on your nerves."

"Oh, one of her special things."

"It's called sensory integration dysfunction. But, she's gotten so much better."

"So, is she going to do it?"

"I hope so."

As we pulled into the crowded parking lot, I saw Don and Christiana on the sidewalk in front of the school—far from the track. Don had his hand on Christiana's back and was talking to her. Christiana had her hands over her ears, her head bent down, and she swayed back and forth, a posture that said "Absolutely not!"

As we approached, Christiana ran to me in tears.

"I want to go home!"

I wrapped my arms around her as she butted into my chest, head down.

"Christiana, you've worked so hard for this. And the gun isn't too loud. Have you even heard it yet?"

A pop in the distance and a responding cheer from the crowd on the bleachers answered me.

Christiana bounced up and down and squeezed her hands like a vice around her ears. "I want to go!"

The pop really wasn't loud. In recent months she had handled sounds much louder. I pulled her away from me and bent down to make eye contact with her.

"Christiana, listen to me. You can handle this. I think you're really more afraid of the idea of a gun shot than the actual sound. Please try.

Look, just take your hands off your ears and stand way out here. Think about winning that ribbon. You'd be so proud of yourself."

Don said, "We won't go in right now. Your race is the last one."

"No! I want to go home!" She buried her face and whimpered.

I looked at Don, my face registering a plea of last-resort, and mouthed the word "ice cream?"

He shrugged and nodded.

I rubbed Christiana's back

"OK, listen Christiana, if you will run this race—no matter if you win or not—we'll take you to get ice cream afterward."

The whimpering stopped and her head popped up.

"Any kind I want?"

"Sure."

"After the race?"

"We'll go celebrate!"

Christiana eased her hands off her ears. The gun popped and she flinched, but her hands didn't quite cover her ears. She smiled. "That's not too bad."

Three races later we had inched Christiana closer to the track until we were standing next to the bleachers. Her hands were once again clasped over her ears. The next race we coaxed her up to the chain link fence surrounding the track.

The gun popped again, and Christiana pressed her hands to her ears—but she didn't move away. I peeled back a couple of fingers and leaned near.

"Christiana, the race has started. You can take your hands off for a few minutes. The gun won't go off again until—"

She shook her head. The cheering from the crowds drowned out my speech as a line of children ran by, clad in multi-colored T-shirts.

I held up one finger and pointed to Christiana and then to the in-field. "Your race is after this next one." I wiggled my eyebrows and shot her a toothy grin of light encouragement.

Christiana didn't return my smile. Her brow wrinkled and her eyes grew wide.

"You'll be fine."

The gun popped. Christiana flinched and stepped back from the fence. The roar from the crowd made me want to cover my own ears.

The announcer called, "All four hundred meter runners please go to the center of the field."

"This is it."

Christiana shook her head.

I turned her toward me and looked into her eyes. "You can do this Christiana. Remember—ice cream."

"OK."

I led Christiana to the gate and nudged her forward, accompanied by cheers of "Good luck" from her Papa and sister. Then Don, Hannah, and I circled around the crowded bleachers and reemerged on the other side near the starting line. I sighted Christiana; she was standing at the starting line on the innermost lane. Her gaze was fixed on the track and her hands were pinned firmly over her ears, but nonetheless, there she stood. The starter raised the gun. Christiana squeezed her eyes shut.

"Pop!"

The line jumped forward. Christiana sprang into action a half-dozen feet behind the field. Her hands came off her ears and she fell into her long-legged stride. I whistled and clapped. She was off!

Christiana ran the race. We celebrated over that fifth-place ribbon like it was an Olympic gold medal. And, in truth, that green fifth-place ribbon meant the first-place award for courage . . . and the power of ice cream.

Reflections

While running the race of faith, certain aspects of the Christian life unnerve us, hinder us from living for God in the joyful freedom of an avid runner. God understands that this is not an easy race and tells us to take courage from the example of those who have finished this race before us. It can be done with God's help!

Prayer

Dear God, help me to identify the things in my life that weigh me down in my relationship to you. Give me courage to face whatever is keeping me from running with freedom. Forgive any sin that shackles me. Heal any wound that disables me. Bear any infirmity that causes me to be weak and afraid. I am resting in you, Lord, as I run. Dear heavenly Father, help me hear your cheers of loving encouragement this day. Thank you. Amen.

As a Little Child

At that time Jesus said, "I praise you, Father, Lord of heaven and earth, because you have hidden these things from the wise and learned, and revealed them to little children. Yes, Father, for this was your good pleasure.
—Matthew 11:25–26

CHRISTIANA LEANED against my shoulder. "Mommy?"

I whispered back the answer to her unspoken question, "You'll do fine, Christiana. It's normal to be nervous when you're getting up in front of lots of people."

From the bench behind the lectern, I scanned the familiar faces of our four-hundred-plus congregation. "You've practiced the verses and you're ready."

I smiled at her, my precious little girl, eleven years old, yet socially and emotionally several years younger. She had insisted on asking to read Scripture at church, even though she wasn't quite graduated from speech therapy. So we had practiced, oh yes, practiced every day that week, the "eyu" sound in "yoke," the "rrrrs," in "earth" and "children." Even if she didn't get it exactly right, they would understand her. Most everybody who attended our traditional service had been in the church for years; probably most already knew these verses.

The organ music stopped and the pastor welcomed the congregation. Christiana fiddled with the paper that held her verses, rapidly flipping the upper corners with her index fingers. I stilled her hands and the rattle. The pastor then signaled the congregation to stand for the first hymn. We stood, and I followed along the words in the hymnal with my finger, but Christiana didn't attempt to sing. She stared at all the people.

She grabbed onto my arm. "I don't want to."

As I answered I kept smiling and didn't look directly at Christiana, hoping I'd appear to still be singing as I spoke. "Christiana, really, you're going to do just great." I had thought ahead to the possibility that she'd be too scared, and I'd decided that if Christiana froze up I would read the Scripture for her. But I hadn't made my plan known to Christiana, as it would only give her a convenient way out of the jitters.

The song ended and the congregation sat down. "OK, Christiana, it's time," I whispered.

I set down the hymnal and handed her the sheet of verses. She looked at me wide-eyed. Putting my hand on her back, I steered her toward the lectern. She paused, staring at the sea of smiling faces. I rubbed her lower back in encouragement.

Christiana raised up the sheet and began to read in enunciated, staccato syllables, "To-day's Gos-pel read-ing is from Matthew 11:25 to 30."

> "At that time Jesus said, 'I praise you, Father, Lord of heaven and earth, because you have hidden these things from the wise and learned, and revealed them to little children. Yes, Father, for this was your good pleasure . . .'"

Christiana continued but I hung on that thought; Jesus reveals the truth to little children—reveals himself. Like many of the Christian university professors and professional ministers in our congregation, I was intent on learning *about* God, on seeking to be wise in the Lord—not bad things. But then the voice of this child, my child, God's child, broke through my impassioned seeking and turned my attention upward from *knowing* about Jesus to simply *seeing* Jesus' face, like a little child looking for love, looking for relationship—looking for him. I hadn't heard it really before now. The Spirit whispered, beckoning me to draw near through Christiana's soft voice. The shift in attention had taken only a moment. Christiana had not faltered in her reading.

". . . All things have been committed to me by my Father. No one knows the Son except the Father, and no one knows the Father except the Son and those to whom the Son chooses to reveal him.

Come to me, all you who are weary and burdened, and I will give you rest. Take my yoke upon you and learn from me, for I am gentle and humble in heart, and you will find rest for your souls. For my yoke is easy and my burden is light."

The congregation sat in a silence that seemed to me suspended in eternity, in blessed rest, away from the heavy burden of knowing— called today to be little children.

Christiana fingered the paper corners. Her eyes had not left the page since she started. Her closing line: "This is the Word of the Lord."

I joined the congregation, one voice, in liturgical affirmation, "Thanks be to God."

What was the meaning of what she had just read? She sort of knew. She liked the part about a "little child," but how could she know what a blessing she had just been by just being herself, by reading because something inside her said *read*. She didn't have a clue as to the gift she had been to me that morning, and to many others that she and I would hear from in the coming week.

Why had Christiana, my only child in speech therapy, wanted so much to read Scripture? She might have had kind words and hugs in mind for herself, but God knew so much more. I'm thankful she listened and obeyed.

Reflections

As adults we sometimes hesitate to follow the inner leading of the Holy Spirit because we don't see the practical value, or we weigh the investment of our time and energy against the probable—seeable— outcome. As God's children with limited vision and understanding, we seldom will know the full purposes and impact of the work we do in the service of God.

Prayer

Dear God, may I be focused upon you and listen to your voice this day. Help me to obey your leading as worshipful service to you. It is so freeing to trust you with the results of the actions that I take for the sake of serving you! Thank you for working in my life and for working in the lives of all those I love in just the right times and ways. May I rest in the peace and simplicity of being your little child today. Amen.

$\mathcal{I}$T'S NOT FAIR

Be joyful always; pray continually; give thanks in all circumstances, for this is God's will for you in Christ Jesus.

—1 Thessalonians 5:16–18

Keep your lives free from the love of money and be content with what you have, because God has said, "Never will I leave you; never will I forsake you."

—Hebrews 13:5

"MOMMY, CAN I HAVE a piece of cake?" Christiana pointed to the translucent cover of the plastic cake-storage container as if gazing at a hunk of frosted heaven.

It was a couple days after my birthday, and Sunday lunch was almost ready. Christiana had been my helper, setting the table and getting drinks.

I started to resist her sugar craving, but I was tired of refusing her requests for cake—cake for breakfast, cake for snack, cake for dessert after every meal. The cake was in its last round anyway. We had all eaten plenty of cake.

"Sure, Christiana. Why don't you divide the cake into five pieces for each of us to have for dessert."

"Really?"

"Why not? You'll be the cake lady today."

Christiana popped the top off the cake plate and grabbed a knife.

I called the family and we all sat down to our Salisbury steak and mashed potatoes.

Fifteen minutes later, Nathaniel headed for the dishwasher with dirty plate in hand. "Time for cake!"

"I'm not quite finished yet," I said, "but if y'all are done, go ahead. Christiana is the cake lady today. She's going to serve us our cake."

Christiana brought the cake over to the table. She had done a fairly good job of making equal portions, but two pieces were noticeably larger.

"Whose are these?" I asked.

"Those are for you and Papa."

Don took his cue and lifted one of the larger pieces onto a plate. "Thank you. I think I'll eat in the office." He exited.

Christiana served herself and then forked two pieces onto plates and passed them to her siblings.

Hannah scowled at Christiana. "Your piece is bigger than mine."

I glanced at the servings. "Not very much bigger, Hannah. I'll let you be the cake lady next time."

"But it's not fair!"

My least favorite mantra. I picked up my lunch plate and headed for the sink. "Hannah, you don't want fair—trust me. If you really want fair, you'd never have cake, except maybe once in your lifetime. Our whole family would live in a one-room house with a dirt floor, and we'd eat food like rice or corn tortillas twice a day and be thankful for that."

Hannah slouched down into her chair as she shoveled her cake into her mouth. My lesson in global perspective had not done the job.

I picked up the cake plate and placed it on the kitchen counter. Nathaniel, having inhaled his cake, left. Christiana eyed the remaining piece. I wondered if I should put it under lock and key to thwart her temptation.

"You know Jesus told a story about this 'unfair' thing," I said. "A master hired a bunch of men to work for him early in the morning. He agreed to pay them a certain amount and . . ."

Hannah sighed. Not Bible story time either.

"Well, anyhow, it's a good story and at the end the master says, 'What is it to you if I am generous with others?' You haven't been mistreated, Hannah." No light of recognition from Hannah, but an idea—

"Christiana, is this *my* piece of cake?"

Christiana nodded.

"And I can do whatever I want with my piece of cake. Eat it now; eat it later; whatever, right?"

"Yes."

I served my piece of cake onto a plate. "Hannah, I give you my piece of cake." I placed the plate in front of my grumpy nine-year-old. "Enjoy!"

Hannah's eyes opened wide. "Really?"

"Sure."

"What?!" Christiana exploded from the kitchen to my side. "But, that's not fair!"

"You said the cake was mine to do with what I wanted. I didn't take your piece of cake did I?"

"No, but—"

"Well, then—"

"Thanks, Mama!" Hannah stacked my plate on top of the crumbs she'd been picking at and took a big bite.

Christiana tugged on my arm. "Give me some, too!"

"Christiana, as the cake lady you divided the cake however you wanted. What difference is it to you, then, what I do with *my* cake? Are you hungry?"

"But—"

"Let me know if there's something you *need* and I'll be sure you get it."

Christiana marched across the kitchen and slammed the door on her way out.

I sat down next to Hannah, who was a good third of the way through her grace cake. "So, Hannah, a minute ago you were very concerned about the cake situation being fair. Is it fair now?"

Hannah stopped chewing and looked at me as if I were speaking a foreign language.

"I'm serious. I want to know. Were you really concerned about being fair or did you just want what you want, sort of being selfish? If you *really* want things to be fair, shouldn't you be splitting the rest of that cake between Christiana and Nathaniel?"

Hannah sighed and shook her head. "All right." Her voice held the annoyance of a picnicker conceding her due to the ants. "Get me a plate and I'll give them each another bite."

Reflections

We are so blessed! I know a single mother who lives every day in a very difficult situation. She's raising two boys, one of which is a high-need, ADHD, diabetic. She works hard hours as a waitress. The boys' father is in prison, providing no support either financially or emotionally. When her sons start whining about how little they have materially, she gets out the newspaper and finds a story or two about someone much worse off than they. Her motto is "Gratitude, forbearance, and love will bring us through."

Prayer

Dear God, help me to recognize how you have blessed me so that I will be overflowing with gratitude. I know that things—the stuff of this life—are not really important, but sometimes I get caught up just like a child in wanting what I want, comparing myself and my circumstances to others' instead of keeping my eyes on you. Help me remember that the greatest unfairness of all time was when Jesus, who was completely without sin and was perfect in love, paid the consequences and bore the guilt and shame of my sin. Thank you for not making life fair for me, but instead blessing me with your living, loving presence. Help me to learn contentment in all circumstances so that your peace and joy will rule my heart and mind. In Jesus' precious name, Amen.

ETERNITY IN THE FLESH

Peace I leave with you; my peace I give you. I do not give to you as the world gives. Do not let your hearts be troubled and do not be afraid.

—John 14:27

As the Father has loved me, so have I loved you. Now remain in my love. If you obey my commands, you will remain in my love, just as I have obeyed my Father's commands and remain in his love. I have told you this so that my joy may be in you and that your joy may be complete. My command is this: Love each other as I have loved you.

—John 15:9–12

CHRISTIANA FLOPPED down on the couch. "I want to go!"

I sat next to her. "Christiana, I need to go by myself this time. You have school this week and Mamaw needs my help. I wouldn't have time to be with you and give you attention anyway, and Mamaw wouldn't either."

Christiana didn't handle sudden change well. My grandma was dying, and I'd decided to leave on Sunday afternoon and drive part of the eight hours to Alabama to be with her. This sudden development rattled Christiana's sense of routine and security.

"I want to be with Mommy. I want to go!" She wrapped her arms across her chest and punctuated her passion by stomping her feet.

"You don't even know Great Grandma Clemens that well,

Christiana. We aren't sure how long she'll live, honey. I don't think you'd enjoy sitting by her bedside with us, and that's just what we'll be doing until she dies and goes to be with Jesus. . . ."

Christiana sniffed; tears ran down her cheeks. "I want to be with Mommy. I don't want you to go."

"Oh, sweetie."

Don sat down on the other side of Christiana. "Christiana, you may not go with Mom. It isn't an option. Hey, we'll go out to eat and you can pick. We'll have a good time here." He smiled at her and brushed the hair away from her forehead.

"No! I want to go! I want to be with Mommy! My kitty died and Grandma Boggs."

She was working her way into a panic. Christiana didn't handle loss well either, even at twelve years old. I believed it was partly on account of her autism. Her thinking was concrete, and if something like souls and heaven weren't evident in the physical world then it wasn't real to her. So, to her, death was final—no souls lived eternally, no heaven existed. She liked the stories about heaven and God and Jesus, but when it came to having faith and hope in them I'm not sure that she could imagine such a reality.

She hadn't been all that attached to the cat, but she grieved it every time she faced a loss. And although she had loved Grandma Boggs, Grandma had lived far away and so hadn't been a daily part of Christiana's life. Otherwise her life had been fairly free of loss. But death frightened Christiana, and so Great Grandma Clemens's imminent passing had unglued her.

"Christiana, look, I hope to be back by the end of the week, we're not real sure yet, of course, but—"

"Are you going to die?"

Her question, the tremor in her voice, attested to the depth of her anxiety. I never wanted to promise my children anything I knew might not be true. The world was not a perfectly safe place. I wanted to tell her Jesus would be with me and with her no matter what happened, and that *if* something happened to me. . . . No, that wouldn't go over well. In her panic she'd hear only that something *was* going to happen to me. I swallowed, praying inwardly, "Dear God, may this be true."

"No, sweetie. I'm not planning on it. I'll be back just as soon as I can, and you can talk on the phone with me every day."

A new wave of tears and pounding feet refused my offer. "I want to go!"

Don looked at me and shook his head. "You probably should get going. We'll be all right."

"I love you, Christiana." I kissed her forehead and walked away to the sound of her wails.

Tears ran down my cheeks as I drove out of town headed south. "Dear God, when I face death I cling to the hope of eternal life beyond this world. I know that you love me and I trust you, and so I 'grieve with hope.' But my sweet Christiana doesn't get it. How can I help her feel safe, Lord? What can I say? What example can I give?"

"Perfect love casts out fear." The Scripture came to my mind in answer.

"Yes, Lord, I try to love her all I can. But how will that help her deal with loss? What will happen to her when Don and I are gone?"

The answering voice wasn't audible, but the words reverberated in my mind with the clarity of a promise: "There will *always* be someone in my church to love Christiana. She will know my love through my people."

The heavy anxiety I had been carrying for Christiana melted into a flood of tears.

"Thank you, Lord. She is yours, and I know that you will never let her go."

Reflections

We all need assurance, hope, and encouragement—especially in times of loss or great need. Although we may not be autistic, we are children who sometimes have difficulty experiencing the assurance of God's unseen presence and promises. At such times, I often pile on top of my anxieties a load of guilt about my lack of faith. God understands how difficult it is for us humans to experience the reality of the eternal. The apostle Paul, who was wholly dedicated to the Lord, said that "now we see things imperfectly as in a poor mirror" (1 Cor. 13:12 NLT).

We were never meant to travel this path of faith alone. God has given us one another in the church to assure and encourage each other. We need not feel guilty about seeking out a brother or sister in Christ to ask for the assurance of God's love through their caring. Also, we need to encourage and assure one another by telling the stories of how God has been real in our lives. God has made us into one body in Christ that we may be, for each other, eternity with skin on it.

Prayer

Dear God, when I feel anxious or lonely or am hurting, help me always to come to you. Let me know that sometimes I will feel the reality of your loving presence in prayer. At other times, you have provided to meet my needs and be real to me through the lives and love of other Christians. Help me, then, to be your loving presence to others and to share with them how you are real in my life. Amen.

No GREATER LOVE

Greater love has no one than this, that he lay down his life.

—John 15:13

How great is the love the Father has lavished on us, that we should be called children of God! And that is what we are!

—1 John 3:1

This is how God showed his love among us: He sent his one and only Son into the world that we might live through him. This is love: not that we loved God, but that he loved us and sent his Son as an atoning sacrifice for our sins.

—1 John 4:9–10

THE STORIES IN THIS book reflect only a few of the wonderful lessons, the eternal insights, the emotional healing and growth God has given Don and me through parenting our children. As parents, God has taught us how to defer our wants for another's need and how to find joy in another's happiness. Born with our first child was a God-given parental love that prays and works and anguishes for another's good over many months and years with little earthly reward. Our lives were our own before children; we had time to plan our schedules and orchestrate even our spiritual lives. And then God gave us kids and began teaching us the greatest lesson of love—to lay down our lives for our precious ones.

Just as our children don't have to do anything to earn the gifts of our time and energy and love for them, our heavenly parent, in an astonishing gift of grace, laid down his life for us through Jesus Christ. To the extent that we realize this ultimate parental love of God, we will experience deep in our hearts "how great is the love the Father has lavished on us, that we should be called children of God!"

Foreword by Gloria Gaither

CHILDREN
Are A
BLESSING
from the
LORD

Learning God's Wisdom Through Our Children

Tamara Boggs

*W*hile quiet moments for parents may be rare, this collection of thirty-one touching reflections reminds weary moms and dads that every day, whether frenzied or serene, is filled with demonstrations of God's blessing . . . for those who are watching.

Each brief devotional centers on lessons gathered from the daily grind of life and points to this truth: When we see God's wisdom through the unique lens of a child's life, we will be reminded that children are indeed a blessing from the Lord.

"This book of moments from my friend Tamara is not for 'mommies only.' It is for anyone who longs for fresh insights from the heart of a seeker in sneakers."

—GLORIA GAITHER

"Young moms will find practical help and lots of encouragement in these pages."

—BOB LEPINE
FamilyLife Today